MARTINIQ __
TRAVEL GUIDE
2026

Essential Information to Discover the Island of
Flowers in the eastern Caribbean Sea Like a
Local, Complete with Insider Tips and a Detailed
Map

Theresa J. Bennett

ABOUT THE AUTHOR

Theresa J. Bennett is a distinguished travel author and seasoned explorer whose passion lies in igniting a sense of adventure in others. Her expertly written travel guides serve as trusted companions for those seeking not just to see the world, but to truly experience it. With every page, Theresa encourages readers to turn ordinary vacations into unforgettable journeys filled with cultural richness and personal discovery.

Having spent years traveling across some of the world's most mesmerizing locations, Theresa brings a wealth of knowledge and firsthand experience to her work. Her guides reflect a genuine reverence for global cultures and a keen eye for hidden gems, those special places that many overlook but few forget. From iconic sites to secret corners, she equips travelers with the insight and confidence to explore deeply and meaningfully.

Praised for her evocative storytelling and precise attention to detail, Theresa J. Bennett's writing captures the essence of each destination. Her books go beyond logistics and itineraries; they offer immersive experiences, combining practical travel tips with authentic cultural context that enriches every step of the journey.

Whether you're a seasoned traveler or planning your very first trip, Theresa's guides offer inspiration, clarity, and a personal touch that makes every voyage feel like a guided adventure with a trusted friend. With Theresa J. Bennett as your guide, every trip becomes an opportunity to connect, grow, and see the world through a new lens.

TABLE OF CONTENTS

MAP

Chapter 1

Welcome to Martinique

The Island at a Glance

Martinique is an island of striking contrasts, a place where Caribbean vibrancy merges seamlessly with French elegance, and where lush rainforests rise up from the shoreline to meet volcanic peaks that watch over tranquil bays. Situated in the heart of the Lesser Antilles, Martinique is a French overseas region, which means visitors will find a fascinating blend of West Indian spirit and European refinement. It offers a unique experience for travelers who seek not only sun and sea but also culture, history, and an ever-changing landscape. At a first glance, Martinique may seem small on the map, stretching only about 70 kilometers from north to south, but the island holds an astonishing variety of scenery, activities, and traditions that make it one of the most captivating destinations in the Caribbean.

The northern half of Martinique is dominated by dramatic volcanic terrain, the most famous feature being Mount Pelée, a towering volcano whose eruption in 1902 devastated the town of Saint-Pierre. Today, its verdant slopes and misty forests provide endless opportunities for hikers and nature enthusiasts. This region is characterized by rugged coastlines, black sand beaches, cascading waterfalls, and dense vegetation where tropical flowers flourish. For those who crave a sense of adventure and discovery, northern Martinique feels like stepping into a natural sanctuary, untouched and unhurried, where the island reveals its wild side.

By contrast, the southern half of the island offers a different personality. This region is defined by calm turquoise waters, pristine white sand beaches, and postcard-perfect views that attract beach lovers and families alike. Towns such as Les Trois-Îlets, Le Diamant, and Sainte-Anne are hubs of activity where travelers can swim, snorkel, or simply enjoy the gentle pace of island life. The south is also where Martinique's most popular resorts and seaside accommodations are located, catering to those who wish to pair natural beauty with comfort and convenience. It is here that the rhythm of the Caribbean feels most alive, with waterfront restaurants serving fresh seafood, lively beach bars, and colorful markets that showcase the island's artisanal spirit.

At the center of the island lies Fort-de-France, the bustling capital that serves as Martinique's cultural and economic heart. The city is a reflection of the island's dual identity: French sophistication coexists with Afro-Caribbean vibrancy. Visitors strolling through Fort-de-France encounter historic architecture, lively squares, traditional Creole eateries, and boutiques filled with Parisian-inspired fashion. It is also the best place to experience the daily pulse of Martinican life, whether through open-air markets filled with spices and tropical fruits, or through art galleries and museums that highlight the island's rich cultural heritage.

Martinique's charm lies not only in its landscapes but also in its people and traditions. The local population embodies a diverse heritage, blending African, European, and indigenous influences into a culture that is expressed through music, dance, food, and festivals. Creole, the local language spoken alongside French, carries the stories of this heritage, and its rhythm can be heard in traditional songs and expressions. From the upbeat sounds of zouk music to the colorful parades of Carnival, the island's cultural calendar is alive with events that reflect both its Caribbean roots and French connections.

Another defining characteristic of Martinique is its deep relationship with the sea. Surrounded by the warm waters of the Caribbean, the island is an ideal destination for snorkeling, diving, and sailing. Coral reefs teem with marine life, while fishing villages along the coast preserve traditions that have shaped island life for generations. For many visitors, simply gazing out at the horizon where the ocean meets the sky is enough to feel the serenity that Martinique so effortlessly offers.

Economically, Martinique is supported not only by tourism but also by its world-renowned rum production. The island is home to a long tradition of distilling rum made from pure sugarcane juice, known as rhum agricole. This spirit is more than just a drink; it is part of Martinique's identity, with distilleries dotting the landscape and offering visitors a chance to taste the island's craftsmanship in every sip. Paired with the island's culinary scene, which blends French refinement with Caribbean spices, Martinique becomes a paradise for food and drink enthusiasts.

When travelers first set foot on Martinique, they quickly realize that this island is not a one-dimensional destination. It is not solely about relaxation on sun-drenched beaches, nor is it exclusively about hiking through tropical forests. Instead, Martinique is a place where every turn reveals a new surprise, whether it is a secluded cove, a lively street market, or a breathtaking mountain view. Its diversity allows each visitor to create their own version of paradise, whether that means an adventure-filled holiday, a cultural journey, or a tranquil retreat.

To see Martinique at a glance is to understand that it is more than an island; it is an experience layered with history, culture, and natural beauty. It captures the essence of the Caribbean while maintaining its French flair, offering travelers a destination that feels both familiar and exotic. With its landscapes divided between rugged wilderness and gentle beaches, its people carrying a proud and diverse heritage, and its traditions enriching every moment spent on the island, Martinique leaves an impression that endures long after a traveler has returned home.

Why Visit Martinique

There are countless Caribbean islands that promise sunshine, beaches, and relaxation, yet Martinique offers something more profound, something that sets it apart as a destination worth traveling across oceans to discover. The reasons to visit Martinique extend far beyond its reputation as a tropical paradise; it is an island where contrasts come together, where every corner tells a different story, and where culture and nature merge into a rich experience that travelers carry with them long after their journey ends.

One of the most compelling reasons to visit Martinique is its dual identity. Unlike many of its Caribbean neighbors, Martinique is both unmistakably Caribbean and distinctly French. As an overseas department of France, it offers the comfort and familiarity of European standards, from well-maintained roads to healthcare and safety, while retaining the warmth, rhythm, and authenticity of the Caribbean lifestyle. This unique balance creates an environment where travelers can sip fine French wine one evening and dance to zouk music under the stars the next. It is a destination that satisfies the traveler who craves diversity, a place where you can have Parisian-style sophistication alongside barefoot island charm.

Martinique also attracts visitors with its extraordinary variety of landscapes. Few islands can boast such a range of natural beauty within such a compact space. In the north, volcanic mountains rise dramatically from the sea, their slopes covered in dense rainforest and alive with tropical birds, exotic flowers, and hidden waterfalls. Hiking trails lead to breathtaking viewpoints, the most famous being Mount Pelée, a symbol of the island's resilience and beauty. In the south, the scenery softens into long stretches of golden and white sand beaches where the waters are calm, clear, and inviting. Each beach has its own personality: some are lively with beachside cafes and water sports, while others are quiet sanctuaries where you might find yourself alone with the sound of waves. The contrast between the rugged wilderness of the north and the tranquil, beach-strewn south makes Martinique a paradise for travelers who do not want to choose between adventure and relaxation.

Beyond its landscapes, Martinique shines in its cultural richness. The island's history has shaped a people and a culture that is diverse, resilient, and creative. African, French, indigenous, and even Indian influences blend together to form a unique identity that is visible in every aspect of life here, from the Creole language to the music that fills the air during festivals. Carnival in Martinique is one of the most colorful and energetic celebrations in the Caribbean, a dazzling display of costumes, music, and dance that invites both locals and visitors to join the party. At other times of the year, smaller festivals highlight traditional music, local cuisine, and the arts, ensuring that no matter when you visit, there is always a celebration of life waiting to be experienced.

Food and drink are also unforgettable reasons to choose Martinique. The island has earned its place as a culinary capital of the Caribbean. Its cuisine is a reflection of its cultural melting pot: French cooking techniques meet Caribbean flavors, producing dishes that are as refined as they are flavorful. Whether you are sampling fresh seafood grilled on the beach, savoring Creole specialties such as accras de morue (cod fritters), or dining on French-inspired gourmet meals, every plate tells a story of history and heritage. To accompany these meals is Martinique's world-famous rum, a spirit deeply embedded in its culture. Distilleries open their doors to visitors, offering tastings that introduce travelers to the island's distinctive rhum agricole, made from fresh sugarcane juice. For lovers of gastronomy and fine spirits, Martinique is a paradise of flavors.

Another reason to visit is the warmth and hospitality of the Martinican people. Travelers often remark that what lingers most in their memory is not just the scenery or the food, but the connections made with locals who welcome visitors with openness and pride in their island. The Creole way of life emphasizes community, rhythm, and joy, and this is something that visitors are invited to share in. Whether through a smile exchanged at a village market, a local guide sharing stories on a mountain trail, or a musician playing in a small bar, the human side of Martinique enriches every journey.

For history lovers, Martinique is also a living classroom. The island has been shaped by centuries of colonialism, slavery, and resilience, and its historic sites tell powerful stories. From the preserved ruins of Saint-Pierre, once destroyed by volcanic eruption, to the monuments and museums dedicated to figures such as Empress Joséphine, who was born on the island, Martinique offers a chance to engage deeply with the past while reflecting on its impact on the present. This connection to history adds depth to a visit, allowing travelers to move beyond the surface beauty of the island and gain insight into the struggles and triumphs that have defined it.

Adventure seekers will find Martinique irresistible. Hiking, diving, sailing, and kayaking are just the beginning of what the island has to offer. Its coral reefs and marine reserves make it a spectacular destination for snorkeling and scuba diving, while its interior landscapes are filled with trails that challenge both experienced trekkers and casual walkers. The island's unique geography means that in a single day you could hike through a rainforest in the morning, swim in turquoise waters by the afternoon, and enjoy live music in a seaside town by nightfall. This ability to combine so many experiences in one trip makes Martinique a dream destination for those who want variety in their travels.

Finally, Martinique is a destination that offers authenticity. While it has the comforts of modern tourism, it has not been overrun by mass development. Villages retain their charm, traditions remain alive, and the island feels like a place where culture and nature coexist in harmony. Travelers searching for an island that feels both accessible and genuine, refined yet unpretentious, will find Martinique to be exactly that.

In short, the reasons to visit Martinique are as layered as the island itself. Its beauty lies in its diversity—of landscapes, of people, of flavors, and of traditions. It is an island that offers more than just relaxation under the sun; it invites you to explore, to taste, to listen, and to feel. Whether you come for the beaches, the mountains, the rum, the music, or the culture, you will leave with the sense that Martinique is not just a place you visited but an experience you lived. It is this combination of qualities that makes Martinique not only worth visiting but worth returning to, again and again.

When to Go

Choosing the right time to visit Martinique is one of the most important steps in planning your journey, as the island's atmosphere and experiences shift subtly with the seasons. While Martinique enjoys warm temperatures and sunshine year-round thanks to its tropical climate, the interplay of weather patterns, cultural events, and visitor crowds means that each season offers a slightly different version of the island. Understanding these variations allows you to decide not just when the flights are cheapest or when the skies are clearest, but when the island will provide the type of experience that best matches your vision of a Caribbean escape.

The most popular time to visit Martinique falls between December and April, when the island enjoys its dry season. This period, often referred to as the high season, is characterized by consistently warm weather, lower humidity, and refreshing trade winds that sweep across the island. Temperatures during these months typically range between 23°C and 29°C, creating ideal conditions for outdoor activities such as hiking Mount Pelée, exploring lush rainforests, or spending long days on the beaches. The sea is calm and inviting, making it perfect for snorkeling, diving, and sailing trips. Because these months coincide with winter in Europe and North America, many travelers escape colder climates to bask in Martinique's sunshine. The demand, however, means higher prices for flights and accommodations, as well as more crowded beaches and towns. If you don't mind a livelier atmosphere and are willing to plan ahead for reservations, this is the perfect time to experience the island at its most vibrant.

February and March deserve special mention within this high season because they bring Martinique's famous Carnival celebrations. Carnival is a highlight of the cultural calendar, drawing both locals and visitors into days of music, parades, dancing, and elaborate costumes. Streets in Fort-de-France and other towns come alive with infectious energy as people celebrate with traditions that blend African, French, and Creole influences. For travelers who want more than just beaches and sunshine, visiting during Carnival provides a chance to immerse yourself in Martinique's culture and feel the island's spirit at its fullest. Of course, this also means more crowds and even higher demand for accommodations, so planning well in advance is essential if you want to be part of this unforgettable celebration.

After April, the weather transitions into what is often called the shoulder season, covering May and June. During these months, Martinique becomes quieter as visitor numbers drop, yet the climate remains pleasantly warm. Rain showers become more frequent, but they are often brief and followed by sunshine, making it possible to enjoy outdoor activities without disruption. The island is particularly lush and green at this time of year, as the rainfall nourishes its tropical flora. Travelers who prefer fewer crowds, lower accommodation rates, and a more relaxed pace may find this period ideal. It is also an excellent season for food lovers, as local markets are overflowing with fresh fruits such as mangoes and guavas, offering a true taste of Martinique's bounty.

July through November marks the wet season, a time when Martinique sees heavier rainfall, higher humidity, and the occasional tropical storm or hurricane, particularly between August and October.

For some travelers, this season may sound less appealing, but it has its own advantages. Prices for flights and hotels are at their lowest, and many of the island's attractions remain open and enjoyable. The rain, while more frequent, often comes in bursts rather than lasting all day, allowing for beach time or sightseeing in between showers. This season also provides opportunities to connect more closely with the local side of the island, as there are fewer tourists and more space to explore towns, markets, and beaches at your own pace. For adventurous travelers who are flexible and seek value, the wet season can still offer a rewarding experience.

September and October are the quietest months of all, as both the weather and the risk of storms keep visitor numbers very low. While some businesses may shorten their hours during this lull, it can be a deeply peaceful time to experience Martinique almost as if it were your own private island. This is the time for travelers who value solitude, who enjoy the sound of rain falling in the rainforest, and who don't mind occasional interruptions in exchange for tranquility.

Ultimately, the best time to visit Martinique depends on the kind of trip you want. If your dream is to lounge on sunlit beaches, hike in crisp air, and join lively crowds, then the dry season from

December to April is your moment. If you want a balance between pleasant weather, fewer crowds, and affordable prices, the shoulder season in May and June may suit you best. And if you prefer to travel more slowly, embrace the unpredictability of tropical showers, and enjoy the island in its quietest form, then the wet season could be your ideal window.

It is also worth considering that Martinique is more than just its weather. Festivals, cultural events, and local traditions can shape your experience as much as the sun and rain. Whether you come for Carnival in February, Bastille Day celebrations in July, or Christmas festivities filled with Creole songs and feasts, aligning your visit with the island's cultural calendar ensures a trip filled with memorable moments.

No matter when you choose to go, Martinique rewards its visitors with something special. Its natural beauty, rich culture, and warm people shine through in every season. While the high season may show the island at its most energetic and the low season at its most tranquil, each period holds the essence of Martinique: an island that always welcomes, always surprises, and always lingers in the heart.

Chapter 2

Need-to-Know Essentials

Language, Currency & Customs

Understanding the basic cultural framework of Martinique, its language, currency, and customs helps transform a trip from a simple vacation into a deeper, more meaningful experience. While Martinique is a small island, it is rich with traditions and practices that reflect both its French administrative identity and its Caribbean soul. Preparing yourself with this knowledge not only makes traveling more convenient but also allows you to connect more genuinely with the people and rhythms of island life.

Language is the first aspect that visitors often notice. As an overseas department of France, Martinique's official language is French, and it is the primary medium used in government, education, business, and signage. Travelers who are comfortable with French will find navigating the island smooth, from reading menus to asking for directions. However, for those who do not speak French, communication may at times present small challenges. English is understood in some tourist-focused areas such as hotels, large resorts, and popular restaurants, but it is far less widespread than in other Caribbean destinations. This makes learning a few key French phrases extremely helpful, not just for practical use but also as a sign of respect that locals deeply appreciate. Even a simple "bonjour" when entering a shop or "merci" after receiving assistance can open doors and create friendlier exchanges.

Alongside French, the island has its own linguistic heartbeat: Martinican Creole (Kréyol). This Creole language is a vibrant blend of French vocabulary, African linguistic influences, and Caribbean rhythms, developed during centuries of colonial history. While French is used in formal settings,

Creole is the language of intimacy, community, and cultural expression. It is spoken in homes, markets, and among friends, and it is deeply tied to Martinican identity. Visitors will often hear it in music, traditional proverbs, and casual conversations. Although learning Creole as a short-term visitor may be challenging, showing curiosity about the language often delights locals, as it acknowledges an essential part of their heritage. In this way, Martinique offers travelers the chance not only to experience French culture abroad but also to encounter the richness of a Creole-speaking community.

The second essential to understand is currency. Because Martinique is part of France and the European Union, the official currency is the euro. This brings certain advantages for travelers: the stability of a strong international currency, easy access to ATMs across the island, and the use of credit and debit cards in most hotels, larger restaurants, and shops. However, visitors should also be prepared for situations where cash is preferred or even required. In small towns, open-air markets, rural guesthouses, or food stalls selling local specialties, euros in smaller denominations are essential. It is wise to carry some coins and small bills for public buses, street vendors, and tipping. ATMs are available in Fort-de-France and larger towns, but in remote areas it may be more difficult to withdraw money, so planning ahead is recommended.

It is worth noting that while prices in Martinique are generally higher than in some neighboring islands reflecting its European connection and import costs, the quality of goods and services often matches the price. Grocery stores and pharmacies, for example, stock familiar European brands, while dining out reflects a fusion of French culinary standards with Caribbean flair. Bargaining is not a common practice on the island, as prices are typically fixed, though at informal markets there may be room for friendly negotiation, especially when buying in bulk.

Understanding customs, cultural norms and everyday etiquette further enriches the travel experience. French influence is evident in the importance placed on politeness and greetings. When entering a shop, office, or even making eye contact with someone in a small town, it is customary to greet them with "bonjour" (good morning or good day) or "bonsoir" (good evening). Failing to greet someone before beginning a conversation may be perceived as impolite. Similarly, when leaving, a "merci, au revoir" is always appreciated. These small gestures go a long way in showing respect for the local way of life.

Another aspect of Martinican custom lies in its blend of French formality and Caribbean warmth. Meals, for example, are not just about eating but about socializing and savoring. Lunch is often considered the most important meal of the day, and many shops and businesses may close during midday hours to allow for this break. Visitors who adjust to this rhythm find themselves more in tune with the island's pace, realizing that Martinique is not a place to rush but to enjoy life's moments.

Religion also plays a significant role in shaping customs. The majority of Martinicans identify as Roman Catholic, and religious festivals and saints' days are widely observed. Churches are central gathering places, especially in smaller communities, and many cultural traditions are intertwined with Catholic rituals. At the same time, Martinique's spiritual life is enriched by Creole traditions and Afro-Caribbean influences, evident in music, dance, and certain community rituals. For visitors, respecting religious spaces and traditions such as dressing modestly when entering a church is important.

Social life in Martinique also reflects the island's cultural diversity. Music and dance are woven into daily life, with zouk and traditional bèlè rhythms often heard at gatherings. Visitors are welcome to join in, as dance is seen not only as entertainment but as an expression of joy and identity. Festivals, from Carnival to smaller village celebrations, often extend invitations to outsiders to participate. Showing enthusiasm and openness to these traditions often leads to warm encounters with locals eager to share their culture.

Finally, understanding customs around tipping and service is useful. Unlike in North America, tipping is not obligatory in Martinique, as a service charge is often included in restaurant bills. That said, leaving a small tip or rounding up the bill is always appreciated as a gesture of gratitude. Taxi drivers, guides, and hotel staff also value small tips, though they are not required.

Altogether, language, currency, and customs are the key threads that weave through daily life in Martinique. Learning a little French or Creole, carrying euros in small denominations, greeting people politely, and respecting the island's rhythms and traditions not only make travel smoother but also create moments of connection. Travelers who embrace these essentials discover that Martinique is not just a beautiful destination but also a welcoming community, one where cultural awareness opens doors to authentic experiences. By approaching the island with respect, curiosity, and a willingness to adapt, visitors are rewarded with encounters and memories that go far beyond the typical Caribbean holiday.

Safety & Practical Tips

Every great journey begins with a sense of security and preparedness. Martinique, while a relatively safe and welcoming island compared to many other destinations, still requires travelers to be mindful of certain practical details to ensure their trip remains smooth and enjoyable. Being aware of safety considerations and everyday travel tips allows you to relax into the island's rhythms and focus on the pleasures of exploration, knowing you are equipped to handle the unexpected.

From a safety perspective, Martinique is generally considered one of the more stable and secure Caribbean destinations. As a French overseas department, it benefits from European standards of law enforcement, healthcare, and infrastructure. Violent crime is rare, particularly against tourists, and most visits to the island are trouble-free. That said, like any destination that attracts visitors, petty crime can occur, especially in busier areas such as Fort-de-France, markets, and popular beaches. Pickpocketing, bag snatching, and theft from rental cars are the most common issues. Travelers are advised to adopt the same precautions they would in any major European city: avoid displaying valuables openly, keep passports and large sums of cash stored safely at your accommodation, and remain mindful of your belongings when in crowded places. Rental cars should never be left with luggage visible inside, especially at beach parking lots, as opportunistic thefts do happen.

The natural environment, while one of Martinique's greatest assets, also presents safety considerations. The island's northern landscapes are dominated by Mount Pelée and surrounding volcanic terrain, which are popular with hikers. Trails can be steep, muddy, and challenging, especially after rainfall. Hikers should wear proper footwear, carry sufficient water, and check weather forecasts before setting out. Sudden changes in weather are common in the mountains, with fog and heavy rain appearing unexpectedly, reducing visibility. Venturing with a guide is recommended for those unfamiliar with the terrain. On the coast, strong currents and rougher seas are more common in the Atlantic-facing northern and eastern shores, while the Caribbean-facing southern beaches are generally calmer. Paying attention to posted warnings and swimming only in designated safe areas is important, especially for families with children. Snorkelers and divers should always use proper equipment, be aware of local conditions, and respect marine life.

Another practical consideration is road safety. While Martinique's road network is modern and well-maintained compared to many Caribbean islands, driving can still be challenging. Roads in the north are winding and narrow, often carved into mountainsides, requiring confidence and attention. Drivers must also adapt to European road rules, which are strictly enforced. Traffic in and around Fort-de-France can be heavy, particularly during rush hours, and parking in urban centers is sometimes limited. Visitors who choose to rent a car should carry their international driver's license alongside their national license and be prepared for roundabouts, steep inclines, and the occasional livestock wandering onto rural roads. Seatbelts are required by law, and driving under the influence of alcohol is heavily penalized.

Health and medical care are areas where Martinique stands out positively. As part of France, the island has a reliable healthcare system with hospitals, clinics, and pharmacies that meet European standards. Pharmacies are well stocked and identifiable by a green cross sign, making them easy to find in towns. Basic over-the-counter medications are readily available, but travelers with specific prescriptions should bring an adequate supply for their stay. Tap water is safe to drink in most places, reducing the need to rely solely on bottled water. Nonetheless, dehydration can be an issue in the tropical climate, especially for those engaging in outdoor activities, so carrying water is essential. Mosquito-borne illnesses such as dengue fever and chikungunya have occurred in the Caribbean, including Martinique, so using repellent and wearing light clothing to minimize bites is recommended, particularly in the rainy season.

Respect for local customs and awareness of cultural etiquette also contributes to a safer and smoother experience. Martinicans value politeness, and greetings are not only courteous but expected. Entering a shop, boarding a bus, or asking for assistance without saying "bonjour" or "bonsoir" may be viewed as abrupt. Visitors who adopt these small but important practices find that locals respond warmly, which in itself enhances safety and ease. When photographing people, especially in rural villages or markets, always ask permission first, as not everyone welcomes being photographed by strangers.

Practical tips for daily life can also make a big difference. Shops, banks, and offices often close for an extended lunch break in the afternoon, a practice influenced by both the French and Caribbean lifestyles. Planning errands, shopping, or traveling around these hours avoids frustration. Sundays are generally quiet, with most businesses closed, although restaurants near tourist areas may remain open. Public transportation is limited outside of major towns, so relying on buses to explore the island may prove inconvenient. Renting a car provides the most flexibility, though boat services to small offshore islets also offer unique opportunities for exploration.

Packing appropriately for the climate is another form of preparation that enhances comfort and safety. Lightweight, breathable clothing is suitable for most of the year, with a light rain jacket or umbrella useful during the wet season. Sturdy walking shoes are essential for exploring volcanic trails and rainforests. Sun protection cannot be overstated: the Caribbean sun is strong, and prolonged exposure without sunscreen, a hat, or shade can quickly lead to sunburn. Travelers planning to swim or snorkel should also bring reef-safe sunscreen to protect the island's delicate marine ecosystems.

For those planning to stay connected, telecommunications are reliable across Martinique, with mobile coverage extending to most inhabited areas. Wi-Fi is available in hotels, cafes, and restaurants, though speeds may vary in rural regions. Having a local SIM card can be useful for navigation and communication, particularly for those driving around the island.

Finally, one of the most practical safety tips is to remain flexible. Martinique is an island that moves at its own pace. Ferries may be delayed by weather, small shops may open later than expected, or rain showers may briefly alter outdoor plans. Approaching these moments with patience and adaptability not only reduces stress but also aligns visitors with the rhythm of island life.

In summary, Martinique is a safe, welcoming, and rewarding destination when approached with awareness and respect. Crime is minimal but requires basic vigilance, the natural environment offers both beauty and challenges, and the culture is warm but expects courtesy. By preparing for these aspects, travelers can enjoy their time without unnecessary worry. With thoughtful planning, an open mind, and a spirit of curiosity, the island becomes not just a destination to visit but a place to experience fully, securely, and joyfully.

Connectivity & Local Etiquette

Staying connected while traveling in Martinique and understanding the nuances of local etiquette are two key aspects that can make your visit smoother, more enjoyable, and far more enriching. While the island offers modern infrastructure, its cultural traditions and social expectations are deeply rooted in both French and Caribbean influences. Knowing how to balance practical needs such as communication with the respect owed to local customs ensures that you move through Martinique not just as a tourist but as a thoughtful guest.

Connectivity in Martinique is generally reliable, reflecting its status as part of France and the European Union. Mobile networks are well established, with coverage extending to most towns, villages, and even many rural areas. Major French providers, such as Orange, SFR, and Digicel, operate on the island, offering strong 4G and increasingly 5G service in urban centers. Travelers from Europe may find that their mobile plans already include Martinique under EU roaming agreements, allowing them to use calls, texts, and data just as they would at home. For others, purchasing a local SIM card is a convenient option, especially for those who plan to rent a car and use navigation apps or wish to stay in touch with family and friends during their stay. SIM cards are widely available in Fort-de-France and larger towns, often requiring only a passport for purchase.

Wi-Fi access is common across Martinique, though the quality varies. Most hotels, resorts, and guesthouses offer complimentary Wi-Fi for guests, and many cafes, restaurants, and public spaces also provide connections. However, speeds can be slower than what travelers might be accustomed to in North America or Europe, particularly outside of the main towns. In remote areas, connections may drop or be unavailable entirely, reminding travelers that they are on an island where natural beauty often outweighs digital immediacy. For many, this becomes part of the charm, an opportunity to disconnect from constant notifications and instead immerse themselves in the slower, more intentional rhythm of island life.

Practical communication tools also help travelers bridge gaps. While French is the primary language of digital services, translation apps can ease interactions, especially in areas less accustomed to English-speaking visitors. Offline maps and phrasebooks are valuable when venturing into rural areas where both connectivity and English comprehension may be limited. Travelers who prepare in advance find that small adjustments like downloading maps before setting out or practicing a few phrases in French go a long way in navigating the island confidently.

Beyond digital connectivity, social connection the way one interacts with locals is perhaps even more important. This is where local etiquette plays a central role. Martinicans, much like the French, place a strong emphasis on politeness and respect in daily interactions. The simplest and most universal rule is to always greet people properly. Entering a shop without saying "bonjour" or approaching someone without an initial greeting can be considered abrupt or even rude. Similarly, when leaving, it is customary to say "merci, au revoir." These small gestures, though seemingly minor, carry significant weight and often set the tone for more welcoming and helpful exchanges.

The pace of life in Martinique also informs its etiquette. The island operates on what is sometimes called "island time," where strict punctuality is not always the priority. Meals may last longer than expected, events may start later than scheduled, and service in restaurants or shops may unfold at a leisurely pace. Visitors who embrace this rhythm, rather than resist it, find that it becomes part of the charm of the island. Patience, rather than urgency, is the cultural norm, and travelers who adapt their expectations accordingly often enjoy a more relaxed and fulfilling stay.

Dress and appearance also reflect local customs. While beachwear is common and accepted at the shore, it is considered inappropriate in towns, markets, or restaurants. Visitors should always wear casual but presentable clothing when moving through public spaces. In more formal settings, such as churches or cultural institutions, modest dress is expected, with shoulders and knees covered as a sign of respect. This awareness of context helps visitors avoid unintended offense and demonstrates cultural sensitivity.

Respect for personal space and community values is another aspect of etiquette worth noting. While Martinicans are generally warm and hospitable, they also value privacy and politeness. Conversations may begin with formalities before moving to more personal topics. Directness, which may be common in other cultures, can sometimes be seen as bluntness here. A respectful approach, accompanied by smiles and courteous language, ensures smoother interactions. Similarly, when photographing people or their property, always ask permission. Many locals are proud to share their culture, but they also expect the courtesy of being asked first.

Etiquette extends to dining and social gatherings as well. Meals are not rushed affairs but moments of connection. Whether you are dining in a family-run restaurant, enjoying Creole specialties at a seaside café, or attending a festival, it is customary to savor food and conversation rather than hurry through. Tipping is modest, as service charges are often included, but leaving a few euros or rounding up the bill is seen as a kind gesture. Sharing appreciation for the food, perhaps with a simple "c'était délicieux" (it was delicious), is always warmly received.

Religion and tradition also influence etiquette in Martinique. As a predominantly Catholic island, Sundays and religious holidays carry special significance. Many shops and services close during these times, and church services are central to community life. Visitors who choose to attend are welcome but should do so respectfully, observing appropriate dress and behavior. Beyond Catholicism, the island's cultural life is infused with Afro-Caribbean traditions and Creole spirituality, which appear in music, festivals, and community rituals. Approaching these practices with openness and curiosity, rather than as spectacles, allows travelers to engage more meaningfully.

Ultimately, etiquette in Martinique is about recognizing that you are entering not just a destination but a living culture. Connectivity may help you find your way on a map or share your photos with friends, but it is the human connections made through greetings, patience, respect, and genuine interest that leave the deepest impressions. The island welcomes visitors who come with humility and enthusiasm, those willing to step into its rhythms rather than impose their own. By doing so, you gain more than convenience; you earn trust, friendship, and the chance to see Martinique not just as a visitor but as a participant in its daily life.

In this way, connectivity and etiquette go hand in hand. Digital tools keep you linked to the wider world, but it is cultural awareness that connects you to Martinique itself. Together, they shape a journey that is not only smooth in practical terms but also rich in meaning and memory.

Chapter 3

Smart Trip Planning

Entry Requirements & Travel Documents

When planning a journey to Martinique, understanding the entry requirements and ensuring that all your travel documents are in order is one of the most important first steps. Martinique is an overseas region of France, and by extension part of the European Union, which means its entry regulations are aligned with French and Schengen rules. For travelers, this offers a mixture of familiarity and specific details depending on nationality. Preparing ahead of time saves you from stress at the airport and allows your trip to unfold smoothly from the very beginning.

For citizens of the European Union, Switzerland, and countries within the Schengen Area, entering Martinique is relatively simple. A valid national identity card or passport is usually sufficient, and no visa is required for short stays. This arrangement reflects Martinique's close integration with France. For these travelers, arriving on the island is much like traveling from one EU country to another, with limited bureaucratic steps. However, passports or ID cards must be valid for the entire duration of the trip, and it is always advisable to check expiration dates well in advance.

For visitors from the United States, Canada, the United Kingdom, and most other countries outside the EU, entry is equally straightforward for short stays. Travelers from these regions do not typically need a visa for visits of up to 90 days within a 180-day period. A valid passport, however, is mandatory. The passport should not only remain valid during the stay but should also have at least six months of validity beyond your intended departure date. Airlines may refuse boarding if these conditions are not met, so checking your passport early in your planning is essential.

For longer stays, such as extended work assignments, study programs, or residencies, a visa or residence permit may be required. In such cases, applications are usually submitted through French consulates or embassies in the traveler's home country prior to departure. The requirements vary depending on the nature of the stay, ranging from work contracts to university admission letters. For retirees or individuals wishing to live in Martinique for several months at a time, additional documentation such as proof of income, housing arrangements, and health insurance may be requested.

Travel documents also extend beyond passports and visas. Airlines often require proof of onward or return travel before allowing boarding. This is particularly relevant for travelers who plan to continue exploring the Caribbean or who have not yet finalized their return itinerary. A confirmed flight reservation helps demonstrate compliance with entry rules. Similarly, travelers may be asked to show proof of accommodation for at least the first part of their stay. Hotel bookings, rental confirmations, or an invitation letter from a host in Martinique are all acceptable.

Health-related entry requirements are another important factor, though they are generally minimal compared to some other destinations. Currently, no mandatory vaccinations are required to enter Martinique from most countries. However, visitors traveling from regions where yellow fever is present must present a valid yellow fever vaccination certificate. Beyond official requirements, it is wise to stay up-to-date with routine vaccinations and consider protections against diseases more common in tropical climates, such as hepatitis A and typhoid. Consulting a travel health clinic before departure ensures you have the right information for your personal circumstances.

Travel insurance is not always a formal entry requirement, but it is strongly recommended. Medical care in Martinique is of high quality, as it is integrated into the French healthcare system, but expenses for non-residents can be significant. Insurance that covers emergency medical treatment, hospital stays, and repatriation provides peace of mind. Additionally, coverage for trip cancellations, delays, and lost luggage helps protect against the unexpected. While you may never need to use your policy, having it in place ensures that a minor mishap does not become a major financial burden.

Travelers from outside the eurozone should also be aware that Martinique uses the euro as its official currency. While this is not directly tied to entry requirements, having a means of financial support is often asked at immigration checkpoints. Credit cards are widely accepted, and ATMs are common in towns, but a small amount of cash is useful for rural areas, markets, or smaller establishments. Immigration officials may occasionally request proof of financial means to ensure that visitors can support themselves during their stay. Bank statements, a credit card, or simply sufficient cash can fulfill this condition.

Families traveling with children must prepare additional documentation. Each child must have their own passport, and depending on the country of origin, additional requirements may apply if a minor is traveling with only one parent or with non-parents. In such cases, a notarized letter of consent from the absent parent(s) may be required, along with copies of identification documents. These measures are intended to prevent child abduction and ensure that minors are traveling with proper authorization. Parents are advised to prepare these documents well in advance, as rules are strictly enforced at international borders.

Beyond formalities, travelers should also consider the practical side of document management. Carrying both physical and digital copies of key documents such as passports, visas, insurance policies, and flight itineraries can be invaluable in case of loss or theft. Storing copies securely on your phone or in cloud storage ensures access even if your bag is misplaced. It is also wise to leave a copy with a trusted friend or family member at home who can assist in emergencies. While Martinique is generally a safe destination, being cautious with documents minimizes stress and disruption should anything go wrong.

It is worth noting that as Martinique is part of the European Union, entry rules are subject to changes in EU policies. For instance, the European Travel Information and Authorization System (ETIAS), expected to be implemented in the near future, will require visa-exempt travelers from outside the EU to obtain pre-travel authorization. This will apply to visitors from countries like the United States, Canada, and the United Kingdom. Though not a visa, ETIAS will function as a security check and must be approved before boarding flights to Martinique. Keeping informed of such updates helps avoid surprises when regulations evolve.

In summary, entry into Martinique is generally straightforward, but success lies in preparation. Valid passports, proof of onward travel, and awareness of health requirements are key to a seamless arrival. Supporting documents such as travel insurance, financial proof, and consent forms for minors provide added protection and reassurance. By organizing these details well in advance, travelers step onto Martinique's shores with confidence, ready to focus not on paperwork but on the beauty, culture, and warmth that await them.

Budgeting Your Stay

Budgeting for a trip to Martinique is an important step in smart trip planning, as it allows travelers to balance comfort, cultural experiences, and financial security while exploring the island. While Martinique is not necessarily the cheapest Caribbean destination, it offers excellent value for those who prepare carefully and tailor their spending choices. By setting a clear budget, visitors can decide how much to allocate toward accommodations, food, transportation, activities, and incidentals, ensuring a stress-free journey that maximizes enjoyment without unnecessary overspending.

One of the most significant expenses for visitors is accommodation. Martinique caters to a wide range of budgets, from luxury resorts and boutique hotels to charming guesthouses, self-catering apartments, and eco-lodges. High-end resorts, especially those with beachfront access, fine dining, and wellness amenities, typically command higher nightly rates that reflect the island's French-Caribbean flair. Travelers seeking a mid-range option can find well-rated hotels and furnished apartments in towns such as Fort-de-France, Trois-Îlets, and Sainte-Anne. Budget-conscious visitors may opt for small family-run inns, Airbnb rentals, or even camping sites that allow them to enjoy the island's natural beauty at a fraction of the price. By considering the type of experience desired, travelers can align lodging costs with their budget, whether prioritizing luxury, convenience, or affordability.

Food and dining are another area where budgeting plays a crucial role. Martinique has a diverse culinary scene influenced by French gastronomy, African traditions, and Creole flavors. Dining out at upscale restaurants, particularly those serving fine French-Caribbean fusion cuisine, can be expensive, especially in resort areas. However, visitors need not rely exclusively on formal dining. Local markets, beachside stalls, and casual eateries known as "lolos" serve generous portions of Creole dishes such as grilled fish, accras (fritters), and colombo curry at much lower prices. Cooking in a self-catering rental or purchasing fresh produce, bread, and cheese from local markets is another way to reduce food costs while still savoring authentic flavors. Balancing indulgent meals at celebrated restaurants with budget-friendly street food or home-cooked options helps stretch dining expenses without sacrificing culinary experiences.

Transportation is an essential aspect of budgeting in Martinique, as the island's attractions are spread out across varied landscapes. Renting a car is often considered the most practical way to explore, offering flexibility and convenience, but it does come with notable costs such as rental fees, insurance, and fuel. Gasoline prices reflect European rates and are generally higher than in many other parts of the world. For travelers seeking savings, carpooling with other visitors, renting smaller vehicles, or choosing accommodations closer to major attractions can help reduce expenses. Public transportation in Martinique is limited but inexpensive, with buses and shared taxis serving certain routes between towns. However, schedules can be irregular, and routes may not reach more remote beaches or hiking areas. For those on tighter budgets, combining occasional car rentals with selective use of buses and taxis can balance cost with accessibility.

Activities and excursions can also impact a traveler's budget depending on the type of experiences desired. Organized tours, such as guided hikes through rainforests, day trips to neighboring islands, or boat excursions to hidden coves, can be pricey but often deliver unique insights and convenience. Independent exploration, by contrast, is often less costly. Many of Martinique's highlights, such as its stunning beaches, hiking trails, and coastal viewpoints, can be enjoyed freely or for a small entry fee. Cultural experiences, including local festivals, open-air music events, and village markets, often provide authentic encounters with minimal or no cost. Travelers can prioritize a few special splurges such as a rum distillery tour, scuba diving adventure, or sailing trip while filling the rest of their itinerary with budget-friendly outdoor exploration and self-guided cultural activities.

When creating a budget, it is also wise to account for incidental costs that may not be immediately obvious. Travel insurance, while sometimes overlooked, is a recommended expense to protect against medical emergencies, cancellations, or lost belongings. Tipping is not mandatory in Martinique as service charges are often included in restaurant bills, but leaving small tokens of appreciation for exceptional service is customary. Shopping for souvenirs, local crafts, or bottles of Martinican rum may also add to expenses, and setting aside a portion of the budget for these purchases prevents overspending at the end of the trip.

Currency considerations are straightforward since Martinique uses the euro. Travelers from the eurozone enjoy the convenience of avoiding exchange rates and currency fees. Visitors from outside the eurozone, such as the United States or Canada, should monitor exchange rates before traveling and consider using credit cards with minimal foreign transaction fees. ATMs are widely available in towns and cities, but it is advisable to carry some cash for rural areas, markets, or small vendors that may not accept cards. Having a strategy for managing money on the island whether through prepaid travel cards, budgeting apps, or a dedicated spending account adds structure to daily expenses and helps keep finances under control.

Seasonality also plays a role in budgeting. High season in Martinique generally runs from December through April, when weather conditions are most favorable. During this time, accommodation prices rise sharply, flights may be more expensive, and availability is limited. Travelers willing to visit during the shoulder or low seasons can often find significant savings. May through June and September through November offer lower hotel rates and discounted flights, though travelers should be mindful of hurricane risks during the late summer months. With flexibility, choosing travel dates outside peak season can free up funds for activities or longer stays.

Budgeting is not only about limiting costs but also about aligning spending with personal priorities. For some travelers, allocating more toward accommodations in a beachfront setting may be worth cutting back on dining or excursions. Others may prefer to save on lodging and splurge on immersive cultural experiences or outdoor adventures. Creating a daily spending estimate for categories such as meals, transport, and entertainment helps establish boundaries while allowing room for spontaneity. Flexibility is important, as unexpected opportunities like joining a local festival or stumbling upon a once-in-a-lifetime excursion often make a trip memorable.

In the end, budgeting your stay in Martinique is less about strict restrictions and more about thoughtful planning. The island provides ample opportunities for travelers of all financial backgrounds to enjoy its natural beauty, rich culture, and French-Caribbean lifestyle. Whether traveling on a shoestring or seeking a luxurious retreat, Martinique rewards careful budgeting with experiences that feel both satisfying and authentic. By anticipating expenses, setting priorities, and leaving room for flexibility, visitors can confidently immerse themselves in the island's charm without the stress of financial uncertainty.

Packing for the Tropics

Packing for a trip to Martinique requires a balance of practicality, comfort, and readiness for the island's tropical environment. While it may be tempting to throw a few swimsuits and sandals into a bag, smart trip planning involves preparing for a range of scenarios, from long days in the sun to spontaneous cultural outings, hikes through lush rainforests, and evenings in sophisticated restaurants. Thoughtful packing not only ensures comfort but also prevents unnecessary purchases upon arrival, helping visitors stay within budget while making the most of their Caribbean adventure.

The foundation of tropical packing begins with clothing that suits the island's hot, humid climate. Lightweight, breathable fabrics such as cotton, linen, and moisture-wicking synthetics are essential, as they keep the body cool and comfortable under the Caribbean sun. Loose-fitting shirts, shorts, sundresses, and skirts are staples that allow airflow and reduce discomfort during outdoor activities. It is also advisable to pack several swimsuits, as they will be used frequently when moving between beaches, pools, and water sports. Many travelers prefer quick-dry options, which make transitions from the sea to sightseeing more convenient. A light cover-up or sarong is useful for beachwear, offering both modesty and sun protection when strolling through towns or dining at casual beach cafés.

Sun protection is one of the most critical considerations when packing for Martinique. The tropical sun is strong year-round, and without preparation, travelers may find themselves dealing with sunburn or heat exhaustion. A wide-brimmed hat, sunglasses with UV protection, and plenty of reef-safe sunscreen are non-negotiable items. Lightweight long-sleeved shirts or dresses in breathable fabrics can provide extra coverage for sensitive skin, especially during outdoor excursions. Aloe vera gel or soothing after-sun lotion is also a wise addition, ensuring comfort if sun exposure is more intense than expected.

Footwear should be chosen with versatility in mind. Flip-flops or sandals are perfect for the beach and casual walks, but sturdier shoes are required for hiking and exploring Martinique's rugged natural landscapes. Trails such as those on Mont Pelée or in the Presqu'île de la Caravelle demand supportive footwear with good grip, as terrain can be uneven or slippery after rainfall. Water shoes are also useful for rocky coastal areas, snorkeling adventures, or kayaking trips, where sharp coral or stones may pose a hazard. A balance of open and closed footwear ensures travelers are prepared for both relaxation and adventure.

Because Martinique combines laid-back island living with French elegance, packing for evenings requires some attention to style. While casual attire is perfectly acceptable in many settings, certain restaurants, bars, or cultural events may call for a slightly more refined appearance. A few smart-casual outfits, such as collared shirts, lightweight trousers, or stylish dresses, are ideal for dining out or attending festivals. Travelers need not bring formal attire, but clothing that feels a step above daytime beachwear ensures comfort and confidence in social or urban settings like Fort-de-France.

Beyond clothing, a well-prepared traveler also considers practical accessories. A lightweight daypack or beach bag is indispensable for carrying essentials such as water, snacks, sunscreen, and a camera during excursions. A reusable water bottle is highly recommended, as staying hydrated in the tropical heat is crucial. Many visitors also carry a dry bag to protect valuables from splashes during boat rides or sudden rain showers. Quick-dry towels, insect repellent, and portable phone chargers are other small but important additions that enhance convenience throughout the trip.

Packing for Martinique should also account for the island's lush natural environment, which means insects, particularly mosquitoes, can be an issue, especially in the evenings or near wetlands. Including insect repellent with DEET or natural alternatives like citronella oil can help prevent discomfort. Lightweight pants and long sleeves can also serve as protection during sunset walks or rainforest hikes. These preparations allow travelers to enjoy the island's outdoor wonders without unnecessary interruptions.

Another consideration is health and wellness items. A small first-aid kit with essentials such as bandages, antiseptic wipes, and pain relievers can be extremely useful, especially for those planning active excursions. Prescription medications should always be packed in their original containers and brought in sufficient quantities for the duration of the trip. Travelers prone to seasickness may want to pack remedies, as boat excursions to nearby islets or whale-watching tours are popular activities.

Including hand sanitizer and antibacterial wipes is also practical, particularly when exploring rural areas or busy markets.

Electronics and entertainment can also play a role in packing for Martinique. While many travelers prefer to disconnect and immerse themselves in island life, items such as a camera, waterproof phone case, or e-reader can enhance the experience. Waterproof cameras or GoPros are excellent for capturing underwater life while snorkeling, while binoculars may be appreciated by birdwatching enthusiasts. Since power outages can occasionally occur in the tropics, a small portable power bank ensures devices remain charged when needed most. It is worth noting that Martinique uses European-style plugs (Type C and E) and operates on 220V electricity, so visitors from North America or other regions should pack a travel adapter.

Smart packing also involves preparing for the island's sudden weather shifts. Though the climate is generally warm and sunny, tropical showers can occur, particularly during the rainy season. A lightweight rain jacket or compact poncho is practical and does not take up much space in luggage. Travelers visiting during hurricane season may want to include additional waterproof storage for electronics and important documents, ensuring peace of mind during unpredictable weather.

Finally, travelers should consider their luggage itself. A medium-sized suitcase or durable travel backpack is typically sufficient for most stays, as Martinique's casual vibe does not require excessive clothing. Packing cubes or compression bags can help keep items organized, particularly when moving between accommodations. A smaller carry-on or day bag is useful for short trips or as a convenient way to store essentials during flights and ferry transfers.

In summary, packing for Martinique is about balancing lightness with preparedness. The essentials include breathable clothing, strong sun protection, versatile footwear, and practical accessories that accommodate both beach relaxation and active exploration. By anticipating the island's tropical climate, cultural sophistication, and natural diversity, travelers can arrive well-equipped and confident. Packing thoughtfully not only prevents unnecessary purchases but also ensures that every moment on the island, whether lounging on a sunlit beach or hiking up a volcanic trail, can be fully enjoyed without the stress of missing essentials.

Chapter 4

Getting Around the Island

Public Transportation & Taxis

Getting around Martinique requires some planning, as the island's transportation system does not always operate with the same frequency or convenience that many travelers may expect in larger cities. However, with the right approach, visitors can make full use of public buses, private minibus taxis, and licensed cabs to move between towns, beaches, and cultural sites. Understanding how these systems work, as well as their advantages and limitations, helps travelers navigate the island efficiently while saving money and enjoying a more authentic local experience.

The backbone of public transportation in Martinique is its network of buses and shared minibuses, known locally as "TC" (short for Transport Collectif). These minibuses are typically privately operated and follow established routes connecting Fort-de-France with surrounding towns and villages. They are a popular choice for locals commuting to work or markets, and they provide travelers with an affordable way to explore the island without renting a car. The main bus terminal in Fort-de-France, located near the Pointe Simon area, serves as the central hub from which most routes begin and end. Travelers staying in or near the capital will find it easiest to access these services, but those staying in smaller resorts or rural areas may need to walk or arrange local connections to reach the main routes.

One of the defining characteristics of Martinique's bus and minibus system is its informality. Unlike in many countries, buses do not always operate on strict timetables. Departures are often based on demand, with vehicles leaving once they are sufficiently full. This means waiting times can vary considerably, especially outside peak commuting hours. Travelers using this system must be flexible, patient, and prepared for some unpredictability. While this can be an adjustment for visitors accustomed to punctual schedules, it also offers a glimpse into the relaxed rhythm of island life, where efficiency often takes a back seat to community and conversation.

Fares on minibuses and public buses are generally inexpensive, making them an excellent choice for budget-conscious travelers. Payments are usually made directly to the driver in cash, so carrying small bills and coins in euros is recommended. Routes commonly connect Fort-de-France with major towns such as Le Marin, Sainte-Anne, Le François, and Saint-Pierre. However, buses and minibuses rarely serve beaches directly, meaning travelers often need to walk from the nearest town stop to their final destination. For those seeking to immerse themselves in local culture, riding with everyday commuters and hearing Creole or French spoken around them can be a memorable part of the travel experience.

In addition to buses and minibuses, taxis play an important role in Martinique's transportation landscape. Licensed taxis are widely available in Fort-de-France, particularly around the airport, ferry terminals, and major hotels. Unlike in many other destinations, taxis in Martinique can be relatively expensive, as fares are calculated by distance and time, with surcharges added for nighttime rides, Sunday travel, or journeys that begin at the airport. Because of these higher costs, taxis are often best used for short trips within towns, transfers to accommodations, or when traveling in groups where the fare can be shared.

One important note about taxis in Martinique is that they are not typically hailed from the street, as in large metropolitan areas. Instead, taxis are usually found at designated stands or called in advance by phone. Many hotels, guesthouses, and restaurants can assist in arranging taxi service for guests. For those arriving at the Aimé Césaire International Airport, an official taxi rank is located just outside the arrivals terminal, where licensed drivers wait for incoming passengers. Agreeing on an approximate fare or ensuring the meter is running before departure helps avoid misunderstandings.

Travelers looking for alternatives to traditional taxis may be surprised to find that ride-hailing apps, so common in many destinations, are not widely established in Martinique. This absence makes licensed taxis and private transfer services the primary option for on-demand transportation. Some companies also offer pre-booked shuttles, which can be convenient for airport-to-hotel transfers, particularly for those staying in resorts farther from the capital.

While taxis and buses are the most common means of public transport, ferries also play an important role in getting around, especially when connecting Fort-de-France with the southern towns of Trois-Îlets and Anse-à-l'Ane across the bay. These passenger ferries are fast, affordable, and scenic, often saving time compared to the long drive around the bay. For travelers staying in Trois-Îlets or nearby, the ferry offers a convenient way to access Fort-de-France without navigating city traffic or relying on taxis. The ferry system is also more predictable than buses, with published schedules and frequent departures throughout the day.

Despite the availability of buses, minibuses, taxis, and ferries, it is important to acknowledge the limitations of relying solely on public transportation in Martinique. Services tend to slow down or stop entirely in the evenings, making nighttime outings difficult without a private car or taxi. On Sundays and public holidays, buses often run on very limited schedules or not at all, which can leave travelers stranded if they are not prepared. For this reason, many visitors combine occasional public transport use with rental cars or organized tours, striking a balance between affordability and convenience.

That said, travelers who embrace the challenge of using Martinique's public transportation often find it rewarding. Riding with locals offers a chance to witness everyday island life, whether it's schoolchildren heading home, vendors carrying baskets of produce, or workers chatting on their way to town. Minibuses in particular can provide a lively, community-oriented experience, where drivers and passengers know one another and often engage in friendly conversation. For the adventurous traveler, this form of transportation can be as enriching as the destinations themselves.

In conclusion, Martinique's public transportation and taxi systems are best suited for travelers who value cultural immersion, flexibility, and affordability over speed and predictability. Buses and minibuses offer budget-friendly connections between towns, while taxis provide comfort and convenience, albeit at higher prices. Ferries enhance connectivity around Fort-de-France Bay, giving visitors both practicality and scenic views. By understanding the strengths and weaknesses of each option, travelers can make informed choices about when to use public transport, when to rely on taxis, and when to consider other alternatives. With an open mind and a willingness to adapt to the island's pace, getting around Martinique becomes an essential part of the journey, offering glimpses into daily life and the rhythms that define this Caribbean destination.

Car Rentals & Driving Tips

Renting a car in Martinique is one of the most practical and liberating ways to explore the island. While public transportation and taxis can cover short distances and key routes, they cannot always reach remote beaches, hidden coves, or mountain villages where some of the island's greatest treasures lie. A rental car allows visitors to set their own schedule, discover lesser-known attractions, and travel beyond the main tourist hubs at their own pace. For many travelers, especially those planning to explore the countryside or travel with family, a rental car becomes less of a luxury and more of a necessity.

Car rental agencies are readily available on the island, particularly at Aimé Césaire International Airport in Fort-de-France. This is the most convenient place to pick up a vehicle upon arrival, as the airport houses both major international rental brands and locally owned agencies. Booking in advance is strongly recommended, especially during the high season from December to April, when demand spikes due to the influx of tourists escaping colder climates. Reserving early not only guarantees availability but also provides better rates and a wider choice of vehicles.

When choosing a rental car, it is important to consider the terrain and road conditions in Martinique. While highways and main roads are generally well-paved and maintained, many secondary roads are narrow, winding, and occasionally steep, particularly in the mountainous northern region. For visitors planning to spend time hiking in rainforests or exploring the volcanic landscapes around Mont Pelée, a compact SUV or a vehicle with good clearance can be beneficial. On the other hand, for those primarily staying in coastal towns and driving short distances, a small economy car is perfectly sufficient, easier to maneuver in traffic, and more practical for finding parking in busy areas.

Driving in Martinique follows French rules of the road, as the island is an overseas department of France. Vehicles drive on the right-hand side, and road signs, speed limits, and traffic regulations are consistent with European standards. Speed limits are generally set at 50 km/h in towns, 90 km/h on most main roads, and up to 110 km/h on certain stretches of divided highways. Enforcement of traffic laws is taken seriously, with fines for speeding, seatbelt violations, and the use of mobile phones while driving. It is also mandatory to carry a valid driver's license, vehicle registration documents, and proof of insurance at all times while operating a car. International visitors can usually drive with their home license, though carrying an International Driving Permit alongside it is often recommended for ease of communication with local authorities.

The driving experience in Martinique can be a mix of ease and challenge. Major roads connecting Fort-de-France to southern towns like Le Marin and Sainte-Anne are relatively straightforward, while rural routes in the north can test the patience of even experienced drivers. Roads around the capital are often busy, particularly during morning and evening rush hours, when traffic congestion builds as commuters travel between suburbs and the city center. Parking in Fort-de-France can also be difficult, as spaces are limited and often filled quickly during the day. In contrast, towns in the south and west, while still lively, tend to offer more relaxed driving conditions.

Gasoline is widely available across the island, with service stations located along main roads and in most towns. Prices are regulated by the government, which means costs remain fairly consistent between stations. Many stations operate with attendants who will pump gas for you, adding a touch of convenience. It is worth noting that some smaller stations may close early in the evening, so travelers venturing into remote areas should plan ahead and avoid running low on fuel.

Navigation in Martinique has been made much easier with the widespread use of GPS and smartphone apps like Google Maps or Waze, both of which function well on the island. These tools are invaluable when navigating winding rural roads or finding less-visited beaches tucked away along the coast. Road signs are generally clear, though they are written in French, which may require a bit of adjustment for those unfamiliar with the language.

Travelers renting a car should also be mindful of practical safety tips. While crime against tourists is relatively low, it is always best to avoid leaving valuables visible inside a parked car, especially at beach parking lots or remote hiking trailheads. Choosing secure parking areas or busy lots reduces the risk of petty theft. Seatbelt use is mandatory for all passengers, and child car seats are required for young children, in line with French regulations. Additionally, drivers should be cautious of sudden rain showers, which can make mountain roads slippery, as well as livestock or stray animals that sometimes wander onto rural roads.

For those who prefer flexibility without the full commitment of a rental car, some agencies offer short-term rentals by the day or even a few hours, allowing travelers to take excursions without depending on public transportation. This option is especially appealing for cruise passengers or visitors staying in Fort-de-France who want to explore a particular region of the island before returning to the capital.

Overall, renting a car is one of the best ways to make the most of a stay in Martinique. It opens doors to secluded beaches, historic ruins, rainforest trails, and charming fishing villages that would otherwise be difficult to reach. The freedom to stop at roadside fruit stands, take spontaneous detours, or linger longer at a favorite beach embodies the spirit of slow travel and discovery. With proper preparation, an understanding of local driving customs, and a sense of adventure, navigating Martinique by car becomes not just a method of transportation, but an integral part of the travel experience.

Exploring by Boat or Ferry

Exploring Martinique by boat or ferry offers an entirely different perspective of the island and adds a sense of adventure that goes beyond the roads and trails. Surrounded by the shimmering waters of the Caribbean Sea and the Atlantic Ocean, Martinique is not only a land destination but also a maritime one. For centuries, boats have been a lifeline connecting fishing villages, small offshore islands, and neighboring Caribbean territories. Today, they remain a practical and exciting way for travelers to get around, whether for scenic exploration, leisure excursions, or inter-island travel.

Within Martinique itself, ferries provide an efficient and enjoyable alternative to navigating the sometimes-congested roads around Fort-de-France. A well-developed network of passenger ferries operates between the capital and several southern coastal towns such as Trois-Îlets, Anse-à-l'Ane, and Pointe du Bout. These short ferry rides, often lasting only 15 to 30 minutes, allow travelers to bypass the heavy traffic and winding roads while enjoying fresh sea breezes and panoramic views of the coastline. The ferries are modern, reliable, and affordable, making them a popular choice for both locals commuting to work and visitors heading to beaches, resorts, or dining spots across the bay.

The experience of traveling by ferry is far from being just about convenience. It becomes an introduction to the maritime rhythm of island life. As the boat leaves Fort-de-France, the capital's colorful buildings gradually fade into the distance, replaced by sweeping views of lush hills, volcanic peaks, and stretches of white sand framed by palm trees. Sitting on deck with the wind in your hair, you feel immediately connected to the sea, which has always been central to the island's culture and history.

Beyond local ferries, Martinique's location in the Lesser Antilles makes it an ideal base for exploring nearby islands. Regular ferry services connect Martinique to neighboring destinations such as Dominica, Saint Lucia, and Guadeloupe. For travelers looking to extend their Caribbean adventure, these inter-island ferries provide a scenic, less hurried alternative to flying. The crossing times vary, with shorter trips like Martinique to Saint Lucia taking around 90 minutes, while longer journeys to Dominica or Guadeloupe can last several hours. These routes are operated by modern vessels equipped with comfortable seating and amenities, ensuring that the voyage itself becomes part of the travel experience rather than just a means of transportation.

For those seeking more freedom and personalization, private boat charters are widely available in Martinique. These can range from small motorboats for independent exploration of nearby coves and snorkeling spots to luxurious yachts complete with a crew. Chartering a boat allows travelers to design their own itinerary, whether it be a leisurely day of sunbathing on deck, stopping at hidden beaches accessible only from the water, or sailing along the island's dramatic northern coastline where cliffs rise sharply from the sea. The southern coast, with its calm waters and string of sheltered bays, is particularly popular for such excursions, while the northern coast offers a wilder, more rugged seascape for adventurous sailors.

Catamaran tours are another favorite way to explore Martinique's coastal beauty. These excursions typically last a half or full day and often include snorkeling stops, island hopping to nearby islets such as Îlet Madame or Îlet Chancel, and meals prepared on board. Catamarans, with their spacious decks and smooth sailing style, are especially appealing for groups, families, or couples seeking a blend of comfort and exploration. The opportunity to swim in crystalline waters, spot tropical fish, or even glimpse dolphins adds layers of excitement to the journey.

Traveling by boat in Martinique also offers cultural insight, as fishing remains a vital part of island life. Many small communities still depend on the sea for their livelihood, and visitors can watch fishermen at work or even join excursions that showcase traditional fishing techniques. Some tours combine cultural storytelling with sailing, giving a deeper appreciation of how the island's history, economy, and cuisine are tied to the sea.

Practical considerations for boat travel are worth keeping in mind. Ferry schedules are generally reliable, but they can be affected by weather, especially during the rainy season or periods of high winds. It is advisable to check timetables in advance and purchase tickets early when traveling during holidays or weekends. For inter-island ferries, passengers are typically required to present valid travel documents, such as passports, since these journeys cross international borders. Motion sickness is another factor to consider, particularly on longer crossings. Carrying seasickness medication or choosing seats on deck where the air is fresh can help make the experience more comfortable.

For safety, operators in Martinique maintain good standards, with ferries and excursion boats equipped with life jackets and safety instructions. Travelers should still exercise basic precautions, such as following crew instructions and remaining aware of their surroundings when boarding or disembarking. When chartering smaller private boats, it is important to verify that the rental company is licensed and that the vessel is properly equipped with safety gear.

Exploring Martinique by water is more than a practical way to get from place to place; it is an essential part of embracing the island's identity. The coastline reveals aspects of Martinique that cannot be fully appreciated from the land: sea caves tucked into cliffs, mangrove channels teeming with birdlife, reefs buzzing with marine life, and quiet bays where the only sounds are the waves and the rustle of palm leaves. By stepping onto a ferry, catamaran, or small boat, travelers gain not only mobility but also a deeper connection to the island's rhythm, its history of seafaring, and its ongoing relationship with the Caribbean Sea.

Chapter 5

Where to Stay

Luxury Resorts & Hotels

For travelers who wish to indulge in the highest levels of comfort, sophistication, and refined Caribbean charm, Martinique offers an impressive selection of luxury resorts and hotels that combine world-class service with the natural beauty of the island. Staying at one of these high-end properties is more than just securing accommodation; it is a full experience that seamlessly blends elegance with the unique culture and scenery of the French Antilles. From beachfront sanctuaries overlooking turquoise waters to secluded retreats in lush tropical gardens, luxury lodging in Martinique caters to travelers who want their stay to feel both relaxing and extraordinary.

One of the most sought-after areas for luxury accommodation is Les Trois-Îlets, a resort hub located across the bay from Fort-de-France. Here, visitors will find upscale hotels and resorts positioned along golden-sand beaches with uninterrupted views of the sea. Many of these properties feature direct beach access, infinity pools, and private terraces where guests can watch the sunset over the Caribbean. The atmosphere is cosmopolitan yet relaxed, with facilities that blend tropical architecture such as open-air lobbies, natural wood accents, and lush landscaping with modern amenities expected at a high-end resort. Fine dining restaurants often feature French-Caribbean fusion cuisine, serving delicacies like lobster, fresh mahi-mahi, and gourmet desserts prepared with island fruits. Evening entertainment, whether in the form of live jazz or traditional dance performances, enhances the sense of staying somewhere that is not only luxurious but deeply connected to local culture.

Another popular location for upscale hotels is Pointe du Bout, a lively area that offers both convenience and luxury. This peninsula is home to stylish resorts, boutiques, and a marina where yachts line up against a backdrop of cafes and restaurants. Luxury properties in this area often cater to travelers who want both relaxation and easy access to activities such as sailing, diving, and shopping. Suites in these resorts frequently come with private balconies, spacious living areas, and oceanfront views that elevate the sense of exclusivity. Many resorts also have on-site spas where guests can enjoy treatments that incorporate tropical ingredients such as coconut, sugar cane, and cacao, offering a unique sensory connection to Martinique's natural bounty.

For those seeking something more tranquil and secluded, the northern and eastern parts of Martinique are home to boutique-style luxury retreats that emphasize privacy and immersion in nature. These smaller, often family-run luxury hotels are hidden among lush hillsides, rainforests, or near volcanic landscapes. Guests may find themselves in a villa-style suite with panoramic views of Mount Pelée or a hideaway surrounded by tropical gardens where hummingbirds and butterflies provide the soundtrack. These properties are designed for travelers who value serenity, eco-consciousness, and a personalized approach to hospitality. Some even offer culinary experiences centered on farm-to-table dining, where ingredients come directly from the property's own gardens or from nearby local producers.

Luxury accommodations in Martinique also excel in offering unique experiences that go beyond the room or suite itself. Many resorts arrange private excursions tailored to their guests, such as champagne catamaran cruises, guided hikes through rainforest trails, or private cooking classes with local chefs. Wellness is another cornerstone of luxury stays on the island. Morning yoga sessions overlooking the sea, massages using essential oils made from island plants, and meditation spaces tucked into quiet corners of the property are common offerings. These experiences help transform a stay into a rejuvenating journey, aligning perfectly with the slower rhythms of island life.

Another dimension of luxury resorts in Martinique is the celebration of French-Caribbean culture. Interiors are often decorated with local art, vibrant fabrics, and handcrafted furnishings that highlight Martinique's heritage. Some properties also feature curated art galleries, rum-tasting sessions, or storytelling evenings that introduce guests to the island's history and traditions. This cultural immersion allows travelers to feel not only pampered but also enriched by a deeper connection to the place they are visiting.

Of course, dining is a highlight of luxury accommodation. Many top resorts boast gourmet restaurants where menus change daily to reflect seasonal availability and the freshest catch of the day. Guests may dine al fresco under the stars, enjoy a beachside barbecue, or have a private meal served on their terrace. The wine lists are often carefully curated, featuring both French vintages and Caribbean specialties, while rum bars provide opportunities to sample Martinique's internationally celebrated agricole rums. Culinary artistry becomes a central part of the luxury experience, ensuring that meals are not just sustenance but memorable events in their own right.

For travelers arriving in Martinique for a special occasion whether a honeymoon, an anniversary, or simply a long-awaited escape the island's luxury resorts and hotels are adept at creating customized experiences. Romantic sunset dinners on the beach, private excursions to hidden coves, and suites decorated with flowers and champagne are common touches that elevate such stays. Families, too, can enjoy the luxury sector of Martinique, as many resorts provide child-friendly activities alongside adult-focused relaxation, ensuring that every member of the group feels cared for.

Choosing a luxury resort or hotel in Martinique also means choosing a gateway to some of the island's best beaches and attractions. Many high-end properties are strategically located near golf courses, marinas, or cultural sites, allowing guests to explore without sacrificing comfort. Yet, for many travelers, the resort itself becomes the destination, offering so many amenities and services that there is little reason to leave. Whether lounging by an infinity pool with a Caribbean cocktail, enjoying personalized service at the spa, or savoring exquisite cuisine, guests quickly discover that the essence of luxury in Martinique lies in the harmony between indulgence and authenticity.

In short, luxury resorts and hotels in Martinique cater to those who want their Caribbean experience to be both pampering and immersive. They offer the refined touches of French elegance, the vibrancy of Creole culture, and the serene beauty of island landscapes, all wrapped into one unforgettable stay. For discerning travelers, choosing this level of accommodation ensures that every moment from waking to the sound of waves to ending the day with a rum cocktail under a star-filled sky feels elevated, effortless, and deeply memorable.

Mid-Range & Boutique Options

For many travelers, the ideal accommodation balances comfort, character, and affordability. In Martinique, mid-range hotels and boutique stays offer just that, a perfect middle ground where visitors can enjoy stylish lodgings, authentic cultural touches, and a warm sense of place without the price tag of luxury resorts. These accommodations are often the most rewarding for travelers who wish to connect with the island on a deeper level, since they frequently combine charm, individuality, and attentive service with accessible pricing.

One of the greatest appeals of boutique hotels and mid-range lodgings in Martinique is their diversity in style and atmosphere. Unlike larger chain resorts, these establishments are often independently owned or family-run, which means that no two are exactly alike. Some are set in historic colonial-era buildings that have been lovingly restored, featuring wooden shutters, wrought-iron balconies, and lush tropical gardens. Others embrace a modern Caribbean aesthetic, with sleek design elements, eco-friendly construction, and minimalist décor that lets the island's natural beauty shine through. This variety gives travelers the chance to choose a property that suits their personal preferences, whether they are drawn to heritage charm or contemporary comfort.

Location is another advantage of staying in mid-range or boutique options. Many of these accommodations are strategically placed in lively towns, fishing villages, or quieter coastal stretches, giving guests the opportunity to immerse themselves in the rhythms of local life. For example, boutique hotels in Fort-de-France provide easy access to the capital's museums, markets, and nightlife, while those in Les Trois-Îlets or Le Diamant place travelers just steps away from some of the island's most inviting beaches. Meanwhile, boutique stays nestled in the northern countryside allow guests to explore rainforests, waterfalls, and volcanic landscapes at their doorstep. This variety of settings ensures that travelers can match their stay to their interests whether cultural immersion, seaside relaxation, or nature exploration.

Amenities in Martinique's mid-range hotels often surprise visitors with their quality and attention to detail. While they may not have the sprawling grounds or multiple restaurants of luxury resorts, they typically provide everything a traveler needs for a comfortable and enjoyable stay. Rooms are often air-conditioned and equipped with modern conveniences like Wi-Fi, minibars, and private balconies. Many properties include swimming pools, small fitness areas, or sun decks where guests can unwind after a day of exploration. On-site restaurants, though often smaller in scale, tend to serve delicious Creole and French-inspired dishes that highlight local flavors, giving guests an authentic culinary experience. Some boutique properties even go above and beyond, offering cooking classes, rum tastings, or excursions led by local guides.

One of the defining characteristics of boutique stays in Martinique is the personalized service. Because these properties are generally smaller than large resorts, staff can provide a higher level of attention and care. Guests often find that hosts and employees take time to share recommendations, arrange excursions, or simply engage in friendly conversation about life on the island. This personal touch creates a sense of belonging and community that is often lacking in larger, more impersonal accommodations. For many travelers, this intimacy and authenticity are worth more than any luxury amenity.

Another appealing feature of mid-range and boutique options is their connection to Martinique's culture and environment. Many properties are designed to reflect local identity, incorporating

Creole architecture, tropical landscaping, and island-inspired interior décor. Guests may find rooms adorned with vibrant textiles, art created by local artisans, or furniture crafted from indigenous woods. Some boutique hotels even focus on sustainability, offering eco-friendly amenities such as solar power, rainwater collection systems, and organic toiletries. These efforts not only reduce environmental impact but also align with the growing demand for responsible travel, allowing visitors to support businesses that prioritize the island's long-term well-being.

For travelers seeking romance or intimacy without the expense of high-end resorts, boutique hotels often deliver in unforgettable ways. Small, secluded properties may have just a handful of rooms, creating a tranquil atmosphere perfect for couples. Private terraces overlooking the sea, candlelit dinners under the stars, and cozy hideaways in lush gardens create an ambiance that feels both exclusive and personal. At the same time, mid-range options are also family-friendly, with many offering family suites, connecting rooms, or activities tailored to children, making them a versatile choice for all types of visitors.

Exploring Martinique while staying at a mid-range or boutique property also has a practical advantage:

proximity to local communities. Guests can easily wander into nearby villages, browse colorful markets, or enjoy meals at family-run restaurants that are off the beaten path. This encourages a deeper connection to Martinique's culture and lifestyle, ensuring that visitors experience more than just the polished tourist perspective. The ease of access to authentic experiences often makes boutique stays a highlight of the journey, as guests return home with stories of friendly encounters and hidden gems they might not have discovered otherwise.

Dining at boutique hotels in Martinique can be especially memorable. Unlike larger resorts with extensive buffets, boutique properties often emphasize quality over quantity, focusing on freshly prepared meals that celebrate Martinique's culinary traditions. Guests may enjoy breakfast with homemade pastries, tropical fruits, and locally roasted coffee, followed by dinners that highlight fresh seafood and Creole spices. In some places, chefs will tailor menus based on the catch of the day or seasonal produce, creating a dining experience that feels personalized and dynamic.

The price range for mid-range and boutique accommodations in Martinique is typically accessible to a wide spectrum of travelers. While they are more expensive than basic guesthouses, they remain significantly more affordable than luxury resorts, making them attractive to couples, families, and solo travelers who want comfort without overspending. The combination of value, charm, and personalized service often makes these properties feel like hidden treasures, where the experience outweighs the cost.

In essence, mid-range and boutique accommodations in Martinique represent the island's welcoming spirit and diverse character. They provide a sense of individuality and warmth that appeals to travelers who want more than just a room; they want a memorable experience infused with authenticity, culture, and comfort. Whether staying in a colonial townhouse in Fort-de-France, a chic seaside boutique in Les Trois-Îlets, or an eco-retreat surrounded by rainforest, guests who choose these options will find that they are not only well-rested but also deeply connected to the island and its people.

Budget Stays & Guesthouses

Not every traveler to Martinique is searching for luxury or boutique charm. For many, the priority is affordability paired with authentic experiences, and that is where budget accommodations and guesthouses shine. These stays allow visitors to enjoy the island's beauty and culture without straining their travel budget, proving that Martinique is a destination accessible to a wide range of travelers. From cozy guesthouses run by local families to no-frills inns, budget-friendly accommodations offer not just savings but also opportunities to engage more closely with Martinique's people and way of life.

Guesthouses, in particular, hold a special place in the accommodation landscape of Martinique. Known locally as gîtes, they are often family-owned and operated, with hosts who take pride in welcoming visitors as though they were long-lost relatives. Staying in a guesthouse frequently means more than simply renting a room; it can be an invitation into the rhythms of daily life. Guests may find themselves sharing meals with their hosts, receiving insider tips about nearby attractions, or learning about traditional recipes, crafts, and customs directly from the people who live them. This intimacy and connection often leave travelers with richer, more meaningful memories than those offered by conventional hotels.

Budget accommodations in Martinique vary in style and setting. Some are rustic seaside lodgings, just steps from the sand, where hammocks swing on porches and ocean breezes cool the rooms. Others are located in bustling towns, providing easy access to markets, cafés, and public transportation. In the countryside, travelers can find simple lodgings surrounded by banana plantations, sugarcane fields, or forested hillsides, ideal for those who want peace, quiet, and immersion in the natural landscape. While amenities in budget stays may be basic fans instead of air conditioning, shared bathrooms, or modest furnishings many compensate with charm, character, and unbeatable locations.

For backpackers and independent travelers, guesthouses and budget hotels are especially appealing. They often serve as gathering places for like-minded travelers, creating a communal atmosphere where friendships are easily formed. Shared kitchens are common, enabling guests to prepare their own meals with fresh produce purchased at local markets, reducing costs while also encouraging culinary exploration. For long-term travelers or those on extended island-hopping trips, this ability to self-cater is both practical and budget-friendly.

Though modest in price, budget accommodations in Martinique are far from lacking in hospitality. Many hosts go above and beyond to ensure guests feel comfortable and welcome, offering rides into town, arranging excursions, or introducing travelers to friends and neighbors. These small gestures create a sense of belonging and warmth that larger hotels often struggle to replicate. In fact, many visitors return to the same guesthouses year after year, not only for the savings but because they feel part of a community.

Another advantage of budget stays is the authenticity they provide. Rather than being surrounded exclusively by other tourists, guests often find themselves staying in neighborhoods where locals live, shop, and socialize. This gives visitors an unfiltered view of life in Martinique, from morning walks to the bakery for fresh baguettes to evenings spent in small rum shops enjoying music and conversation. It is a more immersive style of travel that suits those who value cultural experiences over polished luxury.

In terms of dining, guesthouses and budget hotels often offer simple but hearty breakfasts featuring tropical fruits, homemade jams, and strong local coffee. Some provide optional dinners prepared by the host family, giving travelers the chance to taste authentic Creole dishes in a home-style setting. These meals are often a highlight, combining delicious food with warm conversation and cultural exchange. For budget-conscious travelers, this can also be a convenient and affordable alternative to dining out every night.

Eco-conscious travelers may find that many budget accommodations naturally align with sustainable travel values. Smaller guesthouses typically use fewer resources than large resorts, and many rely on local produce, employ staff from nearby communities, and encourage guests to explore the island responsibly. By staying in these types of lodgings, visitors often make a more positive impact on the local economy while minimizing their environmental footprint.

Despite their affordability, budget accommodations in Martinique often surprise guests with thoughtful touches. Rooms may be decorated with vibrant Caribbean colors, adorned with locally crafted furniture, or surrounded by lush gardens filled with tropical flowers and fruit trees. Hammocks and outdoor seating areas are common, providing tranquil spots for reading, relaxing, or watching the sunset. Even without luxury amenities, these simple pleasures contribute to a rich and satisfying experience.

Safety and comfort are also important considerations. While budget stays may lack certain upscale conveniences, most provide secure and welcoming environments. Travelers should always check reviews and choose established guesthouses or inns to ensure a comfortable experience. In many cases, the level of cleanliness and hospitality exceeds expectations, reinforcing the idea that affordability does not necessarily mean sacrificing quality.

For students, backpackers, solo adventurers, and families traveling on a tighter budget, these accommodations make Martinique a far more accessible destination. With the money saved on lodging, visitors can allocate resources to other enriching experiences such as guided hikes in the rainforest, diving excursions, or sampling a wider variety of local cuisine. By balancing affordability with cultural immersion, budget stays ensure that travelers can explore Martinique to the fullest without financial stress.

In essence, budget accommodations and guesthouses in Martinique represent a style of travel rooted in authenticity, connection, and resourcefulness. They offer more than just a place to sleep; they open the door to a way of experiencing the island that is warm, personal, and deeply enriching. For travelers who value meaningful interactions, cultural immersion, and affordability, these stays can provide some of the most rewarding moments of a journey. By choosing them, visitors not only save money but also contribute directly to local communities, creating a travel experience that is both responsible and unforgettable.

Chapter 6

Don't-Miss Experiences

Fort-de-France Highlights

Any journey to Martinique would be incomplete without spending time in Fort-de-France, the island's vibrant capital and cultural heart. This bustling port city, framed by hills and the shimmering waters of the Caribbean Sea, is a fascinating blend of colonial history, modern Caribbean life, and rich Creole traditions. Far more than just a gateway to the rest of the island, Fort-de-France offers travelers a dynamic and layered experience filled with striking architecture, lively markets, colorful streets, and a thriving arts scene. Exploring the city provides a chance to step into the everyday life of Martinique's residents, while also uncovering landmarks and stories that tell of the island's complex past and evolving identity.

One of the most striking symbols of Fort-de-France is the Schoelcher Library, an architectural gem that immediately captures the eye. Designed in the late nineteenth century by Henri Picq and originally built for the 1889 Paris Exposition, it was dismantled and shipped piece by piece to Martinique. Today, the library stands as both a cultural institution and a historical monument, named after Victor Schoelcher, the French abolitionist who played a central role in the abolition of slavery in 1848. Its ornate iron framework, intricate details, and vibrant façade make it one of the city's most photographed landmarks. Stepping inside, visitors find themselves surrounded by a collection of rare books, manuscripts, and artifacts that highlight Martinique's intellectual heritage. For travelers interested in history and architecture alike, the library is an essential stop.

Nearby, the St. Louis Cathedral rises above the city with its striking Gothic Revival architecture. Also designed by Henri Picq, the cathedral is notable not only for its soaring spire and stained-glass windows but also for its resilience. Over the centuries, the church has been destroyed multiple times by earthquakes, fires, and hurricanes, only to be rebuilt each time with greater strength and beauty. The cathedral remains an active place of worship, but it is also an important cultural site that tells a story of perseverance and faith that resonates deeply with Martinique's people.

No visit to Fort-de-France is complete without experiencing the city's Grand Marché, a lively indoor market that bursts with color, energy, and fragrance. Here, visitors encounter a sensory feast: vendors selling spices piled high in pyramids, stalls overflowing with tropical fruits, and shelves stocked with bottles of homemade rum punches and medicinal herbal blends. The atmosphere is one of warmth and welcome, with local women in brightly patterned madras headscarves offering samples of their goods while sharing stories or recipes. It is a place to purchase souvenirs, but also to engage in cultural exchange, whether bargaining for handwoven crafts or learning how nutmeg, cinnamon, and cloves shape Creole cuisine.

Another highlight of Fort-de-France is the Savane Park, a sprawling green space that offers a serene escape from the bustle of the city. Shaded by royal palms and dotted with statues, fountains, and benches, it is a favorite gathering place for locals and visitors alike. The park holds historical significance as well, as it once displayed a statue of Napoleon's Empress Josephine, who was born in Martinique. The statue became a focal point of controversy due to Josephine's association with slavery and colonial exploitation, and in recent years, it was toppled during anti-colonial protests. Today, the empty pedestal serves as a powerful reminder of the island's complex relationship with its colonial past, making the park not only a peaceful retreat but also a place of reflection.

Art and culture enthusiasts will be drawn to the Aimé Césaire Theatre, named after Martinique's most celebrated poet, politician, and philosopher. Césaire was one of the founders of the Négritude movement, which championed Black identity, culture, and empowerment across the Francophone world. The theater is a hub of performing arts, hosting plays, concerts, and festivals that highlight the creativity of Martinique and the Caribbean. Even if travelers do not attend a performance, the building itself and its connection to Césaire's legacy are worth discovering.

History lovers should also take time to explore Fort Saint-Louis, a seventeenth-century fortress that still serves as a French naval base. Overlooking the bay, the fort is one of the most prominent reminders of Martinique's strategic military importance during the colonial era. Guided tours lead visitors through bastions, dungeons, and ramparts, offering not only historical insights but also stunning panoramic views of the city and harbor. Pelicans often nest along the fort's seawalls, adding a natural touch to the historical experience.

Fort-de-France is also a city of rhythms, flavors, and street life. Wandering through its neighborhoods reveals colorful Creole houses, narrow lanes filled with music, and bustling cafés where locals gather to sip ti-punch or strong coffee. Sampling the city's culinary scene is another highlight, with everything from casual food stalls selling accras (crispy cod fritters) to elegant restaurants blending French technique with Caribbean flavors. In the evening, the city comes alive with music, from jazz and reggae to traditional bèlè drumming and dance, offering opportunities to experience Martinique's vibrant performing traditions firsthand.

For those who want a taste of daily life, simply strolling along the waterfront promenade is an experience in itself. From here, one can watch fishermen mend their nets, ferries depart for neighboring islands, and families enjoy the sea breeze. The view of the bay with its turquoise waters framed by hills is unforgettable, particularly at sunset when the city glows with golden light.

In essence, Fort-de-France is not a city to rush through, but rather one to savor slowly. It is a place where history and modernity intersect, where colonial architecture meets lively markets, and where art and politics intertwine with daily Caribbean life. For visitors willing to immerse themselves in its rhythms, Fort-de-France offers some of the most rewarding experiences on the island. By exploring its highlights, whether grand monuments or small everyday details, travelers gain a deeper understanding of Martinique's soul and the resilience, creativity, and pride of its people.

Rum Distilleries & Plantations

One of the most authentic and unforgettable experiences in Martinique is visiting its rum distilleries and plantations. The island is world-renowned for producing some of the finest rums on the planet, and unlike many other Caribbean islands, Martinique has a unique status: it is the only place outside of Europe to hold the coveted Appellation d'Origine Contrôlée (AOC) designation for rum. This recognition, similar to that given to French wines and cheeses, means that Martinique's rums are produced according to strict traditional standards that ensure quality, character, and authenticity. Exploring these distilleries and plantations is not simply about tasting rum; it is about uncovering the deep cultural, historical, and agricultural ties that have shaped Martinique's identity for centuries.

The island's rum story begins with sugarcane, which was introduced during the colonial period and quickly became the foundation of Martinique's economy. Plantations spread across the island, and over time, many shifted from producing raw sugar to crafting rum. Unlike molasses-based rums produced in much of the Caribbean, Martinique specializes in rhum agricole, distilled directly from fresh sugarcane juice rather than byproducts. This gives the rum a grassy, vegetal character that reflects the terroir of the island, much like fine wine expresses the essence of its vineyard. Visiting a rum distillery allows travelers to witness this process firsthand, from the cutting of the cane to the fermentation and distillation that transforms it into a spirit of remarkable complexity.

Among the island's most famous distilleries is Habitation Clément, located in Le François. This estate is more than just a distillery; it is a cultural and historical landmark where visitors can stroll through manicured gardens, admire colonial architecture, and explore a contemporary art gallery that integrates Martinique's creative spirit with its agricultural past. The rum-making facilities themselves provide fascinating insights into the production process, with opportunities to see the fermentation tanks, copper stills, and oak barrels used for aging. Tastings here are a highlight, allowing visitors to compare white, aged, and vintage rums while learning how subtle differences in soil, climate, and technique affect the final flavor.

Another beloved destination is Distillerie Depaz, located on the lush foothills of Mont Pelée near Saint-Pierre. Depaz is known not only for its robust and flavorful rums but also for its spectacular setting. The distillery sits on the site of a plantation destroyed by the catastrophic 1902 eruption of Mont Pelée, which wiped out the city of Saint-Pierre. Rebuilt with resilience, the estate offers sweeping views of the volcano and Caribbean Sea, creating an unforgettable backdrop for exploring the cane fields and production facilities. Walking the grounds here is both a historical journey and a celebration of survival, as the distillery embodies Martinique's strength in the face of natural disasters.

Rhum J.M, located in the verdant north of the island, is another highlight for those interested in both rum and landscape. Tucked into the tropical Carbet Mountains, this distillery is surrounded by cascading streams and fertile soils that give its rum a distinctive, aromatic profile. A visit here often includes guided tours through the fermentation rooms and barrel warehouses, followed by tastings in a setting that feels close to nature. The rich scents of sugarcane and oak fill the air, adding a sensory dimension to the experience that lingers long after leaving.

For travelers who prefer a smaller, more intimate experience, boutique distilleries and artisanal producers scattered across Martinique provide a window into traditional craftsmanship. Places like La Mauny and Trois Rivières allow visitors to get closer to the daily operations of rum-making, often with guides who explain every detail with passion. These smaller estates tend to offer tastings of unique blends not widely exported, giving travelers the chance to discover rare flavors that embody Martinique's rum culture at its most personal.

In addition to distilleries, many estates still preserve elements of plantation life, offering travelers a chance to step back in time. Walking through cane fields, visitors can imagine the grueling labor once performed there and better understand the complex history of colonialism and slavery that underpins Martinique's rum industry. Today, however, these spaces have been transformed into places of education, reflection, and pride, where the traditions of rum production are celebrated as a living heritage rather than a relic of the past.

Tastings are, of course, an essential part of any visit, and Martinique's distilleries take pride in presenting rum as a nuanced and sophisticated drink. White rums, often fresh and fiery, are the base for classic cocktails like the ti' punch, a local favorite made simply with rum, lime, and sugar. Aged rums, matured in oak barrels for years, reveal layers of flavor vanilla, spice, dried fruit, and caramel that rival fine whiskies or cognacs. Enthusiasts will find that each distillery has its own signature style, and sampling across several sites is the best way to appreciate the diversity of Martinique's rum tradition.

Some estates enhance the experience with cultural events, festivals, or food pairings. Visitors might find themselves enjoying rum alongside Creole dishes, such as grilled fish with plantains or spicy accras, which highlight how the spirit integrates seamlessly into Martinique's culinary culture. Seasonal celebrations, such as harvest festivals, bring music, dance, and storytelling into the mix, creating a vibrant atmosphere that transforms a rum tour into a deeper immersion in island life.

Ultimately, exploring Martinique's rum distilleries and plantations is more than just a tasting journey; it is an encounter with the island's history, culture, and natural beauty. It allows travelers to appreciate not only the craftsmanship behind each bottle but also the resilience and creativity of the people who continue to carry this tradition forward. For anyone who wants to understand Martinique at its core, setting aside time to visit its rum estates is a must. Each sip tells a story of the island's soil, its struggles, its artistry, and its pride, making rum one of Martinique's most powerful and unforgettable cultural ambassadors.

Traditional Festivals & Events

Experiencing Martinique at festival time is one of the most rewarding ways to truly feel the island's rhythm and soul. Beyond its beaches, distilleries, and natural beauty, Martinique comes alive through its traditional festivals and events that reflect centuries of cultural blending. These celebrations are not just entertainment but a living expression of the island's Creole identity, fusing African, European, and Caribbean influences into vibrant spectacles of music, dance, food, and storytelling. For travelers, attending one of these events offers an intimate window into the heart of Martinique, where traditions are cherished and joy is shared openly with visitors.

The most famous and unmissable celebration is Carnival, which takes place every year in the days leading up to Ash Wednesday. Martinique's Carnival is one of the liveliest in the Caribbean and is considered unique even among other French-speaking islands. Unlike the polished parades in places like Rio or Trinidad, Martinique's Carnival is raw, creative, and deeply rooted in satire, humor, and social commentary. From Sunday through Ash Wednesday, towns and villages transform into colorful stages, with parades of costumed dancers, pulsating drumming bands, and floats that often poke fun at politics, colonial history, or modern-day social issues. Each day of Carnival has a different theme. On Monday, participants dress in red to symbolize the devil and dance through the streets in a fiery display of energy. Tuesday is reserved for elaborate costumes made with sequins and feathers, showcasing the artistry and imagination of local designers. Finally, on Ash Wednesday, crowds dress in black and white to mourn the effigy of King Vaval, a symbolic figure representing the Carnival spirit. His burning at the end of the festival marks the conclusion of the celebrations and the beginning of Lent. Travelers who attend Carnival will find themselves swept into the frenzy, where everyone, from children to elders, participates with unrestrained enthusiasm.

Another remarkable event is the Fête de la Musique, celebrated each year on June 21. This island-wide music festival, born in France but embraced wholeheartedly in Martinique, transforms towns into open-air concert halls. Musicians, both professional and amateur, set up in squares, streets, and beaches to perform everything from traditional zouk and bèlè to jazz, reggae, and contemporary pop. For travelers, this event is a chance to immerse themselves in Martinique's musical traditions and feel the beating heart of Creole rhythms. The Fête de la Musique captures the island's love for expression and its ability to bring people together through sound and celebration.

For those visiting in May, La Fête de la Canne, or the Festival of Sugarcane, is a rich cultural experience rooted in Martinique's agricultural heritage. This event highlights the importance of sugarcane and rum to the island's history, with demonstrations of traditional cane cutting, music, and tastings of freshly pressed cane juice. It is a celebration of both work and artistry, where travelers can gain a deeper appreciation for how closely agriculture, economy, and culture are tied together on this island.

In December, the island embraces the festive season with Chanté Nwel, or Christmas Carols, which is unlike any Christmas celebration found elsewhere. Instead of solemn hymns, communities gather for lively, rhythmic renditions of traditional French carols infused with Caribbean beats. Groups of musicians and singers, often accompanied by drums and guitars, visit homes and neighborhoods, turning the season into a spirited festival of food, drink, and music. Families prepare Creole dishes such as pâté salé, smoked ham, and boudin, and share them alongside rum punch and sorrel drinks while singing late into the night. For travelers, participating in a Chanté Nwel gathering is a chance to experience the warmth of Martinique's hospitality and its joyful approach to tradition.

The cultural heritage of Martinique is also celebrated in smaller but equally meaningful events. The Festival International de Jazz de la Martinique, typically held in November or December, attracts musicians from across the globe while spotlighting the island's local talent. It takes place in venues ranging from intimate clubs to outdoor stages, blending international jazz with Creole influences. Similarly, the Festival de Fort-de-France in July brings together theater, dance, literature, and music in a month-long celebration of Martinique's cultural creativity. These events are opportunities for travelers not only to enjoy performances but also to engage with local artists who are keeping Martinique's cultural traditions vibrant and evolving.

Another powerful and historically significant commemoration is the May 22nd Emancipation Day, marking the abolition of slavery in 1848. This day is observed with ceremonies, concerts, exhibitions, and reenactments that honor the struggles and resilience of enslaved people. It is a solemn yet uplifting occasion that helps visitors understand the deep historical layers that continue to shape Martinique's identity.

Even in smaller villages, local festivals known as fêtes patronales take place throughout the year, celebrating the patron saints of each parish. These are community-based events where travelers can experience traditional food, games, parades, and music in a more intimate setting. They reveal how traditions are not confined to grand spectacles but are woven into the everyday lives of Martinique's people.

Attending these festivals and events allows travelers to do more than observe; it invites them to participate. Whether it is dancing in the streets during Carnival, singing with strangers at a Chanté Nwel gathering, or tasting Creole delicacies during a village fête, these moments leave lasting impressions of warmth, energy, and belonging. Festivals are when Martinique reveals its truest self, joyful, expressive, and rooted in traditions that continue to thrive across generations.

For anyone planning a trip, aligning a visit with one of these celebrations can turn a holiday into an unforgettable cultural journey. The rhythm of the drums, the laughter of the crowds, the aroma of Creole dishes, and the spectacle of costumes and colors combine to create experiences that are not just seen or heard but deeply felt. To witness Martinique during festival time is to witness an island in its fullest expression of life.

Chapter 7

Beaches & Snorkeling

Best Family-Friendly Beaches

Martinique is blessed with an extraordinary variety of beaches, each with its own personality, character, and natural beauty. For families traveling with children, the island offers a wealth of safe, calm, and welcoming shorelines where both young and old can enjoy the Caribbean Sea without worry. These family-friendly beaches combine shallow waters, gentle waves, nearby amenities, and a relaxed atmosphere, making them perfect for carefree days of swimming, sandcastle building, and snorkeling in shallow lagoons.

One of the most beloved family beaches in Martinique is Anse Mitan, located in the Trois-Îlets area on the island's western coast. Protected from strong currents and trade winds, this beach has calm waters that are ideal for children learning to swim. The sand is soft and golden, offering a safe place for little ones to play while parents relax under the shade of palms or enjoy a meal at one of the nearby cafés and restaurants. Anse Mitan is also known for its gentle snorkeling opportunities close to shore, where children can spot small fish and colorful corals without venturing far. With its central location, good facilities, and ferry access to Fort-de-France, Anse Mitan has become a favorite destination for both locals and visiting families.

Not far from Anse Mitan lies Anse à l'Ane, another excellent beach for families. This stretch of sand is a bit quieter and offers shallow waters that remain calm throughout the year. The atmosphere here is relaxed, with small eateries serving traditional Creole dishes, ice cream, and snacks that children are sure to enjoy. Families often choose Anse à l'Ane for its balance of convenience and tranquility, as it provides the perfect mix of amenities without feeling overly crowded. The beach also has shady spots, making it comfortable for long stays with young children.

For families looking for a more expansive shoreline, Les Salines in the south of the island is a must. Stretching for nearly a mile, this beach is famous for its postcard-perfect scenery, with fine white sand, turquoise waters, and coconut palms swaying gently in the breeze. Despite its popularity, Les Salines remains remarkably family-friendly because of its shallow entry and gentle waves. Children can play safely along the water's edge while parents enjoy the natural beauty of one of Martinique's most iconic beaches. Vendors selling coconuts, fresh juices, and light snacks add to the appeal, ensuring that families can spend the entire day here without having to leave for provisions. Although snorkeling here is less prominent than at smaller coves, the wide sandy shoreline makes it ideal for family picnics, games, and long seaside walks.

For a quieter option, Anse Noire provides a completely different beach experience. Unlike most of Martinique's white-sand beaches, Anse Noire has striking black volcanic sand, which makes it both visually unique and memorable for children. The waters here are calm and clear, offering some of the best easy-access snorkeling on the island. Families often come here to introduce children to marine life, as schools of tropical fish can be seen just a few steps into the sea. The shady trees along the sand provide natural cover, and the intimate setting makes it a favorite for families who prefer a more peaceful environment.

Another good choice for families is Grande Anse d'Arlet, located on the western coast. This long, tranquil beach is known for its calm, crystal-clear waters and its vibrant marine life. Families can swim safely close to shore, while older children and parents can bring snorkeling gear to explore around the rocks where turtles are often spotted. The beach has a laid-back village charm, with small restaurants, bakeries, and shops nearby, making it easy to combine swimming with a relaxed family lunch. Because the water is so transparent, children are often fascinated to see fish swimming around their ankles, which makes every splash in the sea feel like a discovery.

Families seeking even quieter settings might enjoy Pointe Marin near Sainte-Anne. This sheltered bay offers some of the calmest waters in Martinique, with a gentle slope into the sea that makes it especially safe for toddlers. The beach is lined with trees that provide ample shade, and there are beachside cafés offering simple meals and refreshments. Its peaceful character makes it ideal for families who want a safe, stress-free environment where children can play freely while parents enjoy the serenity of the Caribbean.

For a more adventurous family outing, Anse Dufour, which sits right next to Anse Noire, is another excellent choice. This small cove has soft golden sand and shallow waters that are home to turtles, making it one of the best spots to introduce children to snorkeling. The calm, protected bay ensures safety, and the excitement of seeing turtles gliding gracefully through the water often becomes the highlight of a family's trip. The beach itself has a charming, authentic feel, with local fishermen often preparing their boats nearby, adding to the cultural experience.

What makes Martinique's family-friendly beaches truly special is the combination of natural beauty, safety, and accessibility. Whether a family prefers the lively atmosphere of Anse Mitan, the iconic scenery of Les Salines, or the unique snorkeling opportunities of Anse Noire and Anse Dufour, there is always a perfect match. Many of these beaches are located near villages or towns, so families can easily combine a beach day with a cultural experience, sampling Creole food, browsing markets, or enjoying a stroll along a seaside promenade.

Travelers with children will also appreciate how welcoming Martinique's communities are. Locals are accustomed to families spending the day together at the beach, and it is common to see groups of multiple generations enjoying food, games, and music under the palm trees. For visitors, joining in these family-friendly traditions can add another layer of warmth to their beach experience.

When planning a trip, it is helpful to remember that mornings and early afternoons are the best times to visit family beaches, as the waters are at their calmest and the crowds lighter. Bringing along essentials like reef-safe sunscreen, hats, and plenty of water will ensure comfort, while snorkeling gear, beach toys, and a picnic blanket can make the day even more enjoyable.

In Martinique, beaches are more than just places to swim; they are extensions of family life, where laughter and memories are made under the Caribbean sun. For parents seeking safe and beautiful settings where children can play freely and nature can be enjoyed together, Martinique's family-friendly beaches are among the finest in the Caribbean.

Top Snorkeling & Diving Spots

Martinique is a true paradise for lovers of the underwater world, offering some of the most diverse and colorful snorkeling and diving opportunities in the Caribbean. Surrounded by both the calm Caribbean Sea on its western side and the more rugged Atlantic on its eastern coast, the island provides an impressive mix of conditions for underwater exploration. The western coast is generally the most popular for snorkeling and diving because the waters are calmer, clearer, and rich with marine life, while the southern and northern ends of the island add unique ecosystems, volcanic formations, and coral reefs that make the island a remarkable destination for divers of all levels.

One of the most famous spots for both snorkeling and diving is Anse Dufour. This small, sheltered cove with golden sand has gained a reputation as the best place in Martinique to see sea turtles up close. Just a few meters from shore, snorkelers often encounter turtles gracefully feeding on seagrass, completely unbothered by human presence. For children and beginner snorkelers, this makes Anse Dufour an unforgettable introduction to the wonders of the underwater world. The bay also hosts colorful fish, making it a rewarding spot for those who want to enjoy marine life without going far out to sea.

For divers, the deeper parts of the bay offer a chance to observe larger species and rock formations teeming with activity.

Next to Anse Dufour lies Anse Noire, a striking beach of volcanic black sand that contrasts with the turquoise waters. The snorkeling here is superb, with shallow reefs close to the beach and schools of brightly colored fish darting between rocks and corals. The underwater visibility is excellent, making it easy to admire the intricate coral formations and even spot octopuses and lobsters if you are lucky. Anse Noire is also a favorite for freed divers and scuba divers, who can explore further into the bay and enjoy the calm, crystal-clear water that often feels like a giant natural aquarium.

Grande Anse d'Arlet is another top destination for snorkeling and diving enthusiasts. This long sandy beach with calm waters is popular with families, but just a short swim offshore, the snorkeling reveals vibrant coral reefs where parrotfish, angelfish, and trumpetfish can be seen. One of the highlights here is the presence of sea turtles, which are often spotted swimming peacefully near the rocks. For scuba divers, Grande Anse d'Arlet provides access to a variety of dive sites, including reefs, walls, and small caves that harbor a diverse range of marine species.

For those who want to experience something more adventurous, the Diamond Rock off the southern coast of Martinique is a world-class dive site. Rising dramatically out of the sea, this volcanic formation is more than just a striking landmark; it is also a haven for marine life. Beneath the waves, divers can explore underwater tunnels, arches, and steep drop-offs covered in sponges and corals. The currents around Diamond Rock make it more suitable for experienced divers, but the reward is extraordinary encounters with barracuda, jacks, moray eels, and sometimes even nurse sharks. The abundance of marine life, combined with the dramatic underwater topography, has earned Diamond Rock a reputation as one of the most iconic dive sites in the Caribbean.

Another celebrated diving area is around Saint-Pierre, in the north of the island. Known as the "Little Pompeii of the Caribbean," Saint-Pierre was destroyed by the eruption of Mount Pelée in 1902, leaving behind a hauntingly beautiful underwater landscape of shipwrecks. Divers here can explore several wrecks, including cargo ships and steamboats that now serve as artificial reefs brimming with marine life. These wrecks are covered in sponges, corals, and algae, attracting schools of fish and offering an eerie yet fascinating glimpse into the island's history. The waters around Saint-Pierre are relatively calm, making them suitable for divers with different levels of experience, though some deeper wrecks are best explored by advanced divers.

Snorkelers and divers will also enjoy the Presqu'île de la Caravelle on the Atlantic side. While the waters here can be rougher, certain protected coves and reefs provide excellent snorkeling conditions. The marine environment on this side of the island is slightly different, with more rugged corals and different species of fish compared to the Caribbean side. The area is less frequented by tourists, which adds a sense of untouched beauty to the experience. Divers here may also encounter larger pelagic species thanks to the stronger currents.

For those looking for a calm and easily accessible snorkeling site, Pointe Marin near Sainte-Anne is an excellent choice. The shallow lagoon offers calm, transparent waters that are perfect for beginners. While the marine life here is not as abundant as at Anse Dufour or Anse Noire, it is still a wonderful place to introduce children and first-time snorkelers to the joy of exploring the sea. Families can easily spend the whole day here, enjoying both the beach and the gentle underwater adventure.

Advanced divers will also find thrill at Cap Salomon, a site located near Anse d'Arlet. Known for its deep walls and coral-covered slopes, this spot is home to impressive sponges, sea fans, and a wide variety of fish. Because of the depth and currents, it is best suited to experienced divers, but it rewards them with unforgettable scenery and rich biodiversity.

What makes Martinique particularly appealing for snorkelers and divers is not only the richness of its marine life but also the variety of underwater landscapes. From shallow reefs and sandy lagoons to volcanic drop-offs and historic wrecks, the island offers a wide range of experiences that cater to beginners, families, and seasoned divers alike. Visibility is generally excellent year-round, often exceeding 100 feet, and the water temperatures stay pleasantly warm, making it comfortable to spend long hours in the sea.

Snorkeling and diving in Martinique are more than just recreational activities; they are opportunities to discover another side of the island's natural and cultural heritage. Whether swimming with turtles at Anse Dufour, exploring the volcanic formations around Diamond Rock, or uncovering the shipwrecks of Saint-Pierre, visitors find themselves immersed in a world that is as captivating as the landscapes above water. For anyone who loves the ocean, Martinique promises endless underwater adventures that will remain etched in memory long after the trip has ended.

Hidden Coves & Secluded Shores

While Martinique is well known for its lively beaches and popular snorkeling spots, the island also hides a collection of secret coves and secluded shores that provide a very different kind of escape. These places are often less crowded, tucked away behind headlands, mangroves, or cliffs, offering a chance to enjoy the Caribbean at its most tranquil. For travelers who dream of solitude, unspoiled nature, and quiet moments by the sea, Martinique's hidden corners are a treasure waiting to be discovered. Exploring these beaches often requires a little more effort, perhaps a short hike, a drive along winding coastal roads, or even a kayak journey, but the reward is the feeling of being in a private paradise where the only sounds are the waves, the rustle of palm leaves, and the calls of seabirds.

One such place is Anse Trabaud, located on the southeastern coast. Unlike the easily accessible beaches near Sainte-Anne, Anse Trabaud feels much more remote. Reaching it requires navigating a bumpy dirt road or taking a walk from nearby trails, but the effort is rewarded with a long stretch of golden sand backed by dunes and tropical vegetation. The beach is often nearly empty, with plenty of space to spread out and feel alone with nature. The waves here can be stronger than on the Caribbean side, which makes it a favorite for those who enjoy a bit of body surfing or simply the dramatic beauty of the sea. The atmosphere is raw, natural, and completely different from the polished resorts, making it perfect for travelers who want a wilder side of Martinique.

Further north along the Atlantic side, the Presqu'île de la Caravelle also shelters some hidden coves that are rarely visited. Known mostly for its hiking trails and the Caravelle Nature Reserve, this peninsula is also home to tiny bays where the sand is framed by rocky cliffs and mangroves. These spots often require a walk through the reserve, but once there, visitors find themselves in peaceful surroundings, with only the occasional fisherman passing by. Because the waters on this side of the island are rougher, the coves are less suited to swimming but ideal for quiet contemplation, photography, and enjoying the wild coastal scenery.

In the southern part of Martinique, near Sainte-Luce, lies Anse Figuier, a small, protected beach that feels hidden away despite being relatively easy to reach. Nestled in a curve of the coastline, it offers calm waters shaded by palm trees and almond trees, creating a sense of seclusion even when a few other beachgoers are present. While not as isolated as Anse Trabaud, it still maintains an intimate atmosphere. Families often appreciate it for its shallow waters and gentle waves, but couples and solo travelers find it equally inviting for a quiet day of reading, napping, or floating in the sea.

Another gem is Anse Michel, which remains a secret favorite among locals. Located on the Atlantic side, it is known for its shallow turquoise lagoon that stretches out behind a protective reef. Coconut palms line the shore, and the beach often feels deserted compared to more touristic areas. The breeze makes it popular with kite surfers, but the lagoon's shallow water also means you can walk far out into the sea without ever being fully submerged. It is a place where time seems to slow down, and where the connection with the natural rhythm of the island is almost immediate. For those seeking peace, Anse Michel embodies the essence of a hidden Caribbean retreat.

Heading back toward the Caribbean side, Anse Couleuvre in the north is one of the most secluded and striking beaches in Martinique. It is reached only after a winding drive and a short hike through lush tropical forest, which makes arriving there feel like a small adventure. The beach itself is of fine, dark volcanic sand, hemmed in by steep cliffs and rainforest vegetation. The waters here are clear and inviting, though sometimes deeper and with stronger currents, giving it a more dramatic presence. Because of its isolation, Anse Couleuvre is rarely crowded, allowing visitors to enjoy one of the most atmospheric settings on the island in near solitude. It is also a good starting point for those who enjoy combining hiking with beach relaxation, as the trails in the area lead through dense jungle and offer glimpses of waterfalls before descending to the sea.

Equally enchanting is Anse Grosse Roche, tucked away on the eastern side of Martinique. This beach is named after the large rock formation that dominates the shore, creating a rugged and photogenic landscape. Reaching it involves a short walk from the main road, which ensures that it stays relatively quiet compared to more accessible beaches. The sand is golden, the sea a vivid blue, and the whole area feels unspoiled and far from the bustle of busier resorts. Travelers who make the effort to come here are rewarded with a raw and beautiful stretch of coastline, often shared with no more than a handful of other visitors.

For those who prefer to combine seclusion with snorkeling, Anse Dufour, though well known for its turtles, still has a hidden quality in the early morning or late afternoon when most day visitors are gone. At these times, the small bay feels like a private sanctuary, with calm waters reflecting the setting sun and turtles gliding gracefully under the surface. Similarly, Anse Noire, right next door, becomes a hushed and magical place once the day crowds have left, its black sand glowing in the fading light. Both beaches offer that blend of accessible seclusion which is rare and precious.

The allure of these hidden coves and secluded shores lies not only in their beauty but also in the sense of discovery they provide. Many visitors to Martinique never stray far from the most famous beaches, leaving these quieter gems to those willing to explore. Each of these beaches has its own character, from the wild Atlantic coast to the sheltered bays of the Caribbean side, offering different moods for different travelers. Some are dramatic and windswept, others intimate and calm, but all share the ability to make you feel as though you have stumbled upon something secret and special.

For travelers seeking to balance lively cultural experiences and bustling towns with peaceful moments of solitude, these hidden coves are essential stops. They remind you that Martinique is not only about its popular resorts and attractions but also about quiet encounters with nature, where the sea and land meet in perfect harmony. Spending a day at one of these secluded shores often leaves a deeper impression than any crowded tourist spot, offering a memory of Martinique that feels uniquely personal and deeply connected to the island's soul.

Chapter 8

Nature & Adventure

Hiking Mount Pelée

Dominating the northern horizon of Martinique, Mount Pelée is far more than just a mountain. It is a symbol of the island's natural drama, a reminder of its volcanic origins, and a living connection between the lush rainforest and the sky above. Rising to 1,397 meters, Mount Pelée offers not only breathtaking views and challenging trails but also a journey through layers of history and ecology that reveal the island's character in its most raw and compelling form. For those drawn to adventure and the beauty of nature, hiking Mount Pelée is one of the most rewarding experiences Martinique has to offer.

The mountain's notoriety comes from its catastrophic eruption in 1902, which destroyed the town of Saint-Pierre and claimed thousands of lives. This tragic event etched Mount Pelée into the collective memory of Martinique, yet today the volcano is a place of renewal. The surrounding slopes are covered in lush greenery, home to a rich variety of flora and fauna. Ferns, orchids, and mosses thrive in the humid conditions, while tropical birds and butterflies add color and movement to the landscape. Walking through these trails is like entering a living laboratory of nature, where every step brings you deeper into the heart of Martinique's volcanic soul.

Hiking Mount Pelée is not a uniform experience; the mountain offers several different routes, each with its own level of difficulty and unique scenery. The most popular starting point is from Morne Rouge, where the trail climbs steadily through rainforest and cloud forest before reaching the upper slopes. This route provides a balance between accessibility and challenge, making it a good choice for moderately fit hikers. The trail is well marked, though the climb can be steep and slippery in places, especially when mist or rain descends.

Another route begins at Grand Rivière, on the rugged Atlantic coast. This is a more demanding hike, longer and steeper, and often recommended for experienced trekkers. The path winds through dense jungle, crosses streams, and eventually ascends to the summit from a different angle, offering dramatic views back down to the coastline and the fishing village of Grand Rivière. This trail is less frequented, so it provides a greater sense of solitude and adventure, with the reward of reaching the summit feeling all the more earned.

The climb from the Aileron parking area, near Le Morne-Rouge, is perhaps the most direct route. From here, the trail rises quickly into higher altitude vegetation, where the air cools noticeably and the landscape shifts into moss-covered trees and exposed ridges. On clear days, the views expand outward in every direction, revealing the lush valleys of northern Martinique, the shimmering waters of the Caribbean, and even neighboring islands such as Dominica on the horizon. The upper slopes are often wrapped in mist, however, and part of the adventure lies in waiting for the clouds to break, when suddenly the summit appears bathed in sunlight, creating a sense of wonder that few places can rival.

Reaching the summit of Mount Pelée is a deeply satisfying experience, but the journey itself is just as memorable. The trails are alive with sensory details: the damp scent of earth and foliage, the sound of trickling streams, the rustle of palms in the wind, and the occasional cry of a bird echoing through the forest. As hikers gain elevation, the environment changes noticeably. The lowland rainforests give way to montane vegetation, and finally to sparse, windswept plants clinging to the volcanic soil. This gradual shift creates a layered narrative of nature, as if the mountain tells its story through its plants and landscapes.

For many, the physical challenge of the hike is part of the appeal. The paths can be steep, the humidity taxing, and the footing uncertain, especially after rainfall. Yet these difficulties only enhance the sense of accomplishment upon reaching the summit. Unlike a casual stroll on the beach, hiking Mount Pelée demands effort, preparation, and resilience. It is an adventure in the truest sense, where the unpredictability of weather and terrain ensures that no two hikes are ever quite the same.

Once at the top, the views are nothing short of spectacular. The crater itself, evidence of the volcano's fiery past, is a dramatic reminder of nature's power. Surrounding ridges create a rugged skyline, while far below the lush green of Martinique's countryside stretches toward the blue waters of the sea. On rare, perfectly clear days, the panorama extends across the channel to Dominica, giving a sense of the Caribbean's interconnected geography. Even when clouds obscure the view, however, the summit holds its own kind of beauty, with shifting mists creating an atmosphere that feels both mysterious and otherworldly.

The cultural and historical resonance of Mount Pelée adds another layer to the experience. Hiking here is not only about nature but also about reflecting on the island's history, its resilience, and the way people have rebuilt their lives in the shadow of the volcano. Standing at the summit, it is impossible not to think about the events of 1902, yet at the same time, the thriving vegetation and vibrant ecosystems speak of renewal and the power of life to return.

For practical purposes, hikers are advised to prepare carefully before attempting the climb. Good footwear, sufficient water, snacks, and weather-appropriate clothing are essential. The weather on Mount Pelée is notoriously unpredictable; clear skies in the morning can quickly give way to fog, rain, or sudden gusts of wind. It is always wise to start early in the day, both to avoid the strongest midday heat and to maximize the chances of catching clearer conditions before the afternoon clouds roll in.

Guided hikes are available and can enhance the experience by providing deeper insights into the geology, botany, and cultural significance of the mountain. Local guides often share stories about the volcano's history and point out hidden details in the landscape that might otherwise go unnoticed. For those new to mountain hiking, having a guide also adds reassurance and safety.

Ultimately, hiking Mount Pelée is one of the defining adventures of Martinique. It combines physical challenge with natural beauty, history with ecology, and personal reflection with collective memory. Unlike other activities that can be easily replicated elsewhere in the Caribbean, this hike is unique to Martinique, rooted in its volcanic past and lush, mountainous landscape. It is an experience that lingers long after the descent, leaving travelers with both vivid memories of the views and a deeper appreciation for the island's complexity.

For anyone who seeks not just to see Martinique but to truly feel it, to climb above the forests and look out over sea and sky from the island's highest point, hiking Mount Pelée is essential. It is nature and adventure entwined, a journey that speaks to the spirit of exploration and the enduring allure of the wild.

Waterfalls & Rainforest Trails

Waterfalls and rainforest trails in Martinique open a doorway to some of the most enchanting natural experiences the Caribbean has to offer. While the island is celebrated for its golden beaches and turquoise waters, the lush interior tells a completely different story, one of cascading falls, dense foliage, and trails that lead to discoveries far from the coast. Walking these forest paths and hearing the distant roar of water tumbling over volcanic rock is a reminder that Martinique is more than just a sun destination; it is an island alive with natural beauty shaped by both fire and rain.

Among the most famous waterfalls on the island is Cascade Didier, located just outside Fort-de-France. Reaching this gem requires a moderate hike through dense rainforest, where you follow narrow trails shaded by giant trees and overgrown ferns. The sound of trickling streams keeps you company as you make your way deeper into the forest. The trail can be muddy and slippery, but the reward at the end is a refreshing pool at the base of the waterfall where you can cool off in clear, cold mountain water. It feels worlds away from the bustle of the city, and many travelers find the experience to be a highlight of their visit.

Another must-see is Saut du Gendarme, a waterfall tucked into the tropical forest near Fonds-Saint-Denis. It is easily accessible compared to some other falls, making it a popular stop for those exploring the island's northern interior by car. The setting is lush, with thick vegetation framing the cascade, and picnic spots are scattered nearby. Locals often gather here on weekends, creating a lively atmosphere that makes you feel part of the community. This accessibility also makes it a great introduction to Martinique's rainforest landscapes for travelers who may not have the time or ability to take on more strenuous treks.

For a more secluded adventure, the Gorges de la Falaise near Ajoupa-Bouillon offers a thrilling exploration through narrow canyons carved by volcanic rivers. A guided walk takes you along the gorge, often wading through water, before reaching a series of small but dramatic waterfalls where you can swim and relax. It is less about hiking and more about the adventure of navigating a raw natural environment, and it highlights just how diverse Martinique's landscapes can be within short distances. The setting feels almost primeval, with mossy rocks, hanging vines, and shafts of light filtering through the forest canopy above.

Beyond these famous spots, the rainforest itself offers countless trails, many of which pass by lesser-known streams and cascades. The Trace des Jésuites, one of the island's oldest and most historic trails, winds through dense green forest and follows rivers and small waterfalls along the way. It is both a nature experience and a step back in time, as these paths were once used centuries ago by Jesuit missionaries crossing the island. The hike is challenging in parts but deeply rewarding for those who want to immerse themselves in Martinique's interior landscapes.

The rainforest is not only about waterfalls but about the sensory experience it offers. The air is humid and filled with the scent of wet earth and flowering plants. Birds flit among the trees, and the occasional rustle in the undergrowth hints at the presence of small animals. The soundscape is a constant mix of dripping water, insects, and the rushing flow of distant cascades. Walking through these trails, you begin to understand how vital the forest is to the island's ecosystem, feeding rivers that nourish the land and providing habitats for countless species.

Visiting waterfalls and rainforest trails in Martinique requires some preparation, as conditions can be slippery, and the weather can change quickly in the mountains. Proper footwear, insect repellent, and a willingness to get muddy are essential. Many trails are not heavily marked, so joining a guided hike is often the best way to explore safely while learning about the flora, fauna, and history of the areas you pass through. Guides often share stories about medicinal plants, local traditions, and the role of these landscapes in everyday life, adding a cultural dimension to your adventure.

What makes these experiences so special is the contrast they provide to the coastal life of Martinique. One day you may be lounging on a calm sandy beach, and the next you could be swimming beneath a waterfall in the heart of a rainforest. This duality is what makes the island unique: it offers both classic Caribbean relaxation and thrilling natural exploration. For travelers seeking a deeper connection to the island beyond its shores, following the call of rushing water into the forest is an unforgettable way to discover Martinique's wild heart.

Sailing, Kayaking & Outdoor Sports

Sailing, kayaking, and other outdoor sports in Martinique offer travelers a dynamic way to experience the island beyond its beaches and rainforest trails. Surrounded by the Caribbean Sea on one side and the Atlantic Ocean on the other, Martinique's waters are as much a playground as they are a source of livelihood and culture. Coupled with the island's rugged volcanic terrain, rolling hills, and steady trade winds, it becomes an open invitation to both water and land-based adventure. For those who like to balance relaxation with activity, Martinique is one of the Caribbean's most rewarding destinations for outdoor pursuits.

Sailing has long been part of Martinique's heritage, and the island is known internationally for its passion for the sport. The island's strategic location in the Lesser Antilles, combined with favorable wind conditions, makes it an excellent sailing destination. Yachting enthusiasts will find well-equipped marinas in places such as Le Marin, one of the largest yacht harbors in the Caribbean. Here, sleek catamarans, monohulls, and traditional vessels bob in the water, ready to set off for day trips or longer excursions. Travelers can rent a boat with or without a skipper, join a guided sailing tour, or simply admire the bustling life of the marina before heading out on the sea. Sailing along the island's coastline reveals dramatic cliffs, hidden bays, and stunning perspectives on Mount Pelée and the Pitons du Carbet, all best appreciated from the water.

One of the most authentic sailing experiences in Martinique is the yole, a traditional fishing boat that has become a cultural icon. Every summer, the island hosts the Tour de Yoles Rondes, a spectacular sailing race where teams compete in colorful boats that skim across the water. Travelers who visit during this event are treated to a vibrant celebration of local heritage, with music, food, and cheering crowds along the shoreline. While yole sailing is highly technical, some local operators offer opportunities to sail with a crew for a hands-on introduction to this unique tradition. It is not just a sport but a cultural immersion that connects you to the soul of Martinique.

For those who prefer a closer connection to the water, kayaking is one of the best ways to explore the island's coastlines and mangrove ecosystems. The southern part of the island, particularly around Trois-Îlets and Le François, offers calm lagoons dotted with small islets that are perfect for paddling. Gliding across turquoise waters, you can stop at sandbars that emerge at low tide or pull up to uninhabited islets fringed by coral reefs. The Îlets du François, including the famous "Baignoire de Joséphine," are especially popular for kayaking trips, where you can combine paddling with swimming in shallow, crystalline waters that stretch as far as the eye can see.

The mangroves of Martinique provide another kayaking adventure, allowing travelers to navigate winding waterways shaded by tangled roots and overhanging branches. This experience offers both serenity and education, as guides often explain the ecological importance of mangroves in protecting the coastline, nurturing marine life, and filtering the water. Birdwatchers will particularly enjoy these excursions, as the mangroves are home to herons, kingfishers, and other coastal species.

Beyond sailing and kayaking, Martinique's landscapes invite a wide range of outdoor sports for those who crave variety. Windsurfing and kitesurfing are popular on the Atlantic side of the island, where stronger winds and waves create ideal conditions. The beaches of Le Vauclin and Cap Chevalier are particularly well-known among water-sports enthusiasts, with schools and rental shops providing gear and instruction for both beginners and advanced riders. The exhilaration of skimming across the waves with the wind in your sail offers a thrilling contrast to the calm waters of the Caribbean side.

For land-based outdoor activities, Martinique's volcanic terrain provides ample opportunity for exploration. Mountain biking trails wind through the island's interior, taking riders past banana plantations, forested hills, and quiet rural villages. Riders of different skill levels will find routes suited to them, from easier coastal paths to challenging climbs and descents in the north. Adventure seekers may also try canyoning in the island's gorges, where guided tours involve rappelling down waterfalls, sliding along smooth rocks, and swimming through natural pools. It is a sport that blends adrenaline with the island's natural beauty, offering memories that last long after the trip ends.

Even more traditional sports like golf and tennis take on a unique flair in Martinique thanks to the island's stunning scenery. The Golf International de Trois-Îlets, designed by renowned architect Robert Trent Jones Sr., offers an 18-hole course set against a backdrop of the Caribbean Sea. Playing here is as much about the views as the sport itself, and it highlights how outdoor activities in Martinique can seamlessly combine recreation with relaxation.

Outdoor sports on the island are not just about physical activity but about immersion in the environment. Whether it is the spray of seawater on your face as you sail along the coast, the stillness of mangrove waters while paddling, or the rush of adrenaline as you descend a canyon, these experiences bring you closer to Martinique's diverse landscapes. They allow you to see the island from different perspectives above, within, and beyond the shoreline, each one offering its own sense of discovery.

Travelers who come to Martinique seeking adventure will find that the island caters to both the seasoned sports enthusiast and the curious beginner. Professional guides, rental facilities, and training programs make it easy to try something new, while the island's natural conditions ensure that every activity feels rewarding. By blending sailing, kayaking, and outdoor sports into your itinerary, you transform a simple Caribbean holiday into a multifaceted adventure that captures both the excitement and serenity of Martinique's unique character.

Chapter 9

Food, Rum & Nightlife

Creole Cuisine & Must-Try Dishes

Creole cuisine in Martinique is more than food; it is a story told on every plate, a history shaped by centuries of cultural exchange, resilience, and creativity. The island's location in the Caribbean made it a meeting point for peoples and traditions from Africa, Europe, and Asia, and this blend is reflected in its gastronomy. Dining in Martinique is not merely about satisfying hunger but about engaging in a cultural ritual that expresses identity, memory, and hospitality. For travelers, experiencing

Creole cuisine is one of the most rewarding ways to connect with Martinique, and it provides insight into how history and environment have come together to shape local tastes.

At the heart of Martinican cuisine lies the concept of the "Creole table," a fusion of French culinary techniques with African spices, indigenous Caribbean ingredients, and influences from India and the wider world. This creates flavors that are bold, colorful, and full of contrast. Meals often balance the freshness of the sea with the richness of tropical produce, seasoned generously with aromatic herbs and fiery chili peppers. Eating out in Martinique can range from sampling a quick street-side snack to savoring elaborate multi-course meals in refined restaurants, yet in every case, the essence of Creole cooking shines through.

One of the most iconic dishes travelers encounter is accras de morue, small fritters made from salted codfish blended with herbs, garlic, onions, and peppers, then deep-fried to golden perfection. Crispy on the outside and soft inside, accras are usually served as appetizers or street snacks, often accompanied by a spicy dipping sauce. These savory bites are part of everyday life and also feature prominently in festivals, making them a must-try for anyone visiting the island.

Colombo is another cornerstone of Martinican cuisine, a dish that reflects Indian influence on the island. Made with chicken, goat, or fish, Colombo is simmered with a spice blend that includes turmeric, coriander, cumin, cloves, and mustard seeds, giving it a distinctive yellow color and aromatic flavor. The dish is often accompanied by root vegetables like cassava and yams, or sometimes eggplant and zucchini, cooked until tender in the sauce. Unlike a fiery curry, Colombo has a gentle heat balanced with depth, making it both comforting and complex.

Seafood holds pride of place in Martinique's culinary tradition, thanks to the island's abundant coastal waters. Grilled lobster, fresh snapper, and conch prepared in Creole sauce are popular choices. The Creole sauce, made with tomatoes, onions, peppers, garlic, and herbs, is a versatile preparation that can be used with fish, shellfish, or even chicken. Court-bouillon, a type of fish stew, is another specialty. It typically features whole fish simmered in a tangy tomato-based broth spiced with hot peppers and lime, served with rice to soak up the flavorful sauce. Each fishing village has its own variations, and tasting these local renditions offers a window into the island's diversity.

No meal in Martinique feels complete without side dishes that showcase the richness of the land. Rice and beans are staples, often paired with fried plantains, breadfruit, or callaloo, a leafy green vegetable cooked into a thick stew. Manioc, known locally as cassava, is another traditional staple that appears in both savory and sweet preparations. From cassava bread to dumplings added to soups, it reflects the enduring influence of indigenous foodways. Tropical fruits are abundant and add vibrant freshness to the table. Mangoes, guavas, soursop, coconuts, and passionfruit appear in juices, desserts, or simply sliced and eaten fresh. Ti-punch, the national drink, is often paired with such fruits, creating a perfect balance between sweetness and the fiery kick of rum.

Speaking of rum, it is inseparable from Martinican cuisine. The island produces some of the finest agricole rums in the Caribbean, made directly from fresh sugarcane juice rather than molasses. This production method gives the rum a distinctive grassy, herbal character that pairs beautifully with Creole food. Locals often enjoy ti-punch as an aperitif before meals, a ritual that involves mixing white rum with lime and cane syrup to taste. Dining establishments across the island take pride in their rum offerings, sometimes serving aged varieties that have been mellowed in oak barrels. Food and rum together form an essential part of the Martinican lifestyle, and to taste one without the other is to only experience part of the story.

Street food culture is another way to savor Creole cuisine. From roadside stands to beachfront shacks, visitors will find vendors serving grilled fish, chicken skewers, or bokits sandwiches filled with meat or fish inside fried bread. These quick meals are deeply satisfying and give travelers the chance to mingle with locals in a relaxed atmosphere. Markets are also excellent places to discover flavors. The bustling market in Fort-de-France is a sensory experience, with stalls piled high with spices, peppers, tropical fruits, and prepared foods. Walking through the market, you can taste samples, talk to vendors, and learn about traditional recipes passed down through generations.

Desserts in Martinique are another highlight. Flan au coco, a creamy coconut custard, is beloved across the island, as is blancmange, a gelatin-based dessert flavored with coconut milk and spices. Rum cake and fruit preserves also hold a special place, particularly during holidays. Travelers with a sweet tooth will also find delight in fresh fruit sorbets, often sold on the beach in vibrant colors and flavors like guava, tamarind, or passionfruit.

What makes dining in Martinique especially memorable is the context. Meals are often shared experiences, accompanied by music, laughter, and a spirit of togetherness. A simple lunch by the beach with grilled fish and fried plantains can feel as enriching as a fine dining meal in a stylish Creole restaurant. It is this sense of community and celebration that gives Martinican food its soul.

Exploring Creole cuisine in Martinique is not just about tasting new dishes but about understanding the island's history and way of life. The spices that came with Indian laborers, the cod brought by European trade, the African techniques of blending herbs and peppers, and the indigenous reliance on cassava all intertwine in every meal. For travelers, every bite becomes a discovery of the island's past and present.

By indulging in the dishes that define Martinique, from street-side accras to slow-cooked Colombo, you not only satisfy your appetite but also participate in a living tradition. The experience of Creole cuisine extends beyond the restaurant or market; it lingers in memory, encouraging travelers to return again and again to relive the flavors that made them fall in love with the island.

Rum Tasting & Distillery Tours

Rum is more than a drink in Martinique; it is an identity, a proud tradition, and an art form perfected over centuries. The island is considered one of the rum capitals of the world, and its unique style of production known as rhum agricole sets it apart from many other Caribbean islands. Unlike most rums, which are made from molasses, Martinique's rhum agricole is distilled directly from freshly pressed sugarcane juice. This method creates a spirit that is vibrant, aromatic, and deeply tied to the land, as the flavor reflects the terroir, much like fine wine. For visitors, rum tasting and distillery tours are among the most rewarding experiences on the island, offering not only a sensory journey but also a lesson in Martinique's history, culture, and craftsmanship.

The tradition of rhum agricole dates back to the seventeenth century, when sugarcane was first introduced to the island. Over time, small distilleries began experimenting with producing rum directly from cane juice, creating a distinctive style that eventually earned worldwide recognition. In 1996, Martinique's rhum agricole was awarded the coveted Appellation d'Origine Contrôlée (AOC) designation, similar to those held by French wines and cheeses. This means that production is strictly regulated, ensuring authenticity and quality while protecting the island's rum-making heritage. For travelers, this designation also provides assurance that each distillery visit and tasting will reveal something unique and remarkable.

Distillery tours in Martinique combine history, agriculture, and sensory exploration. Each distillery has its own character, shaped by geography, tradition, and innovation. Visitors often begin by walking through sugarcane fields, learning about the varieties grown and the harvesting process. Guides explain how the cane is crushed to extract juice, which is then fermented and distilled to produce rhum agricole. The aging process is another highlight, as barrels of rum rest in cellars for years, developing complexity and depth. Tasting sessions follow, allowing guests to sample a wide range from the grassy freshness of white rum to the smooth elegance of aged varieties.

One of the most renowned distilleries is Habitation Clément, located in Le François. This estate is not only a distillery but also a cultural site with a historic Creole house, lush gardens, and an impressive art collection. A visit here feels like stepping back in time while also exploring the island's artistic spirit. The tour typically includes a walk through the fermentation and distillation rooms, followed by a chance to taste different rums in a scenic setting. The aged varieties in particular, with notes of vanilla, caramel, and oak, leave a lasting impression on visitors.

Another must-see is Distillerie Depaz, located at the foot of Mount Pelée. The volcanic soil enriches the sugarcane grown in this area, giving the rum a distinctive character. The estate is striking, with its beautiful mansion overlooking the Caribbean Sea. A tour here offers insights into how geography influences flavor, and visitors often comment on the fresh, almost floral notes in the rums. Distillerie Neisson, one of the smallest on the island, offers a different experience. Known for its artisanal approach and emphasis on quality over quantity, Neisson produces rums that are highly sought after by connoisseurs. Visiting this family-owned distillery feels intimate and personal, and the tastings highlight the artistry involved in crafting rhum agricole.

Distillerie La Mauny in Rivière-Pilote is another favorite, especially for those who enjoy vibrant, community-oriented experiences. The estate offers train rides around the property, making it fun and accessible for families while still providing detailed explanations of the production process. Tastings here include a wide range of rums, from fresh white varieties ideal for cocktails to complex aged versions meant for slow sipping. Distillerie Saint James, one of the oldest and largest, adds another layer of interest with its museum dedicated to rum and sugarcane history. The scale of this distillery contrasts with the smaller operations, showing visitors the diversity of rum-making approaches on the island.

Tasting rum in Martinique is an education in flavor. White rhum agricole is often described as fresh, grassy, and slightly peppery, making it perfect for cocktails such as the famous ti-punch. Aged rums, known as rhum vieux, offer a different experience, with layers of flavor developed through years in oak barrels. Notes of dried fruit, spices, vanilla, and toasted wood make these rums ideal for sipping slowly, much like a fine cognac. There are also amber rums, which fall between white and aged, offering balance and versatility. For travelers, sampling these different styles side by side reveals the extraordinary range and sophistication of Martinique's rum.

Distillery tours also highlight the cultural role of rum in Martinican society. It is not only a drink but a symbol of hospitality and identity. Sharing a ti-punch is part of daily life, and it is customary for guests to mix their own, adjusting the balance of rum, lime, and sugar to taste. During festivals, rum flows freely, bringing people together in celebration. Distilleries often host events, concerts, or tastings that blend music, food, and drink, offering a joyful immersion in local culture.

Beyond the distilleries themselves, rum tastings can also be found in restaurants, bars, and specialized shops. Many establishments curate rum menus with dozens of varieties, allowing visitors to compare different producers and styles. Bartenders often act as guides, recommending pairings with food or explaining the nuances of each rum. For those who want to bring a piece of Martinique home, duty-free shops and local markets sell beautifully bottled rums, often packaged in decorative boxes that make them perfect souvenirs.

What makes rum tasting in Martinique unforgettable is the sense of connection it fosters. By sipping rhum agricole, travelers engage with the land, the people, and the traditions that shape the island. Each distillery has a story, whether it is about resilience after a volcanic eruption, dedication to family craft, or innovation in blending techniques. These stories come alive during tours, reminding visitors that rum is not just a product but a living heritage.

For anyone traveling to Martinique, visiting at least one distillery is essential, but the experience becomes richer when several are explored. Each estate adds its own perspective, offering a deeper understanding of the diversity and artistry of rhum agricole. Whether wandering through lush estates, learning about fermentation and aging, or savoring a glass of aged rum while overlooking the sea, these tours are journeys of discovery.

Rum tasting and distillery visits ultimately leave travelers with more than memories of exquisite flavors. They offer insight into the island's character, where tradition and innovation coexist, and where the essence of Martinique is distilled in every bottle. For many visitors, this becomes one of the highlights of their trip, an experience that lingers long after they have left the island, inviting them to return and raise a glass once more.

Nightlife & Live Music

Nightlife and live music in Martinique embody the island's rhythm, blending African heritage, French sophistication, and Caribbean vibrancy into evenings that stretch long after the sun has set. For many visitors, the energy of Martinique is not just found on its beaches or in its mountains, but in the music and movement that animate its streets, bars, and open-air venues after dark. Whether you are in the capital Fort-de-France, a coastal town, or a small village where locals gather, nights in Martinique always feel alive with possibility. From zouk and biguine to reggae, jazz, and modern fusion, the sounds of the island offer a cultural immersion as much as they do entertainment.

Fort-de-France is the natural starting point for nightlife, with its mix of chic cocktail lounges, lively dance clubs, and open-air cafés that attract both locals and travelers. The city has long been a hub of creativity and performance, with venues that host everything from jazz ensembles to DJ-led Caribbean beats. Rooftop bars and harbor-front terraces often provide not only drinks and food but also a soundtrack of live music, setting the stage for evenings that can move seamlessly from relaxed conversation to spirited dancing. For those who enjoy a polished night out, the capital offers a cosmopolitan setting infused with the distinct character of Martinique.

Beyond the capital, coastal towns such as Trois-Îlets, Sainte-Anne, and Le Diamant bring a more laid-back approach to evenings, yet the vibrancy remains just as strong. Beach bars along the sand often feature live bands, where the music mixes with the sound of waves, creating a truly

Caribbean atmosphere. These nights feel more intimate, inviting you to dance barefoot in the sand or simply sip a ti' punch while listening to local musicians. The island's smaller communities often host open-air events or fêtes that allow visitors to step into the daily rhythm of Martinican life, where dancing under the stars is as natural as gathering for a shared meal.

Music is at the heart of Martinique's nightlife, and its diversity reflects the island's rich cultural roots. Traditional biguine and mazurka rhythms, brought to life with drums, guitars, and brass instruments, carry the soul of Martinique's Creole heritage. Zouk, a genre born in the French Caribbean, dominates dance floors, with its infectious rhythm and romantic lyrics captivating both young and older audiences. Salsa, reggae, and calypso add to the mix, blending seamlessly into the island's sonic landscape. For visitors, these evenings offer more than just entertainment; they provide an authentic connection to Martinique's history and cultural identity through sound and movement.

Festivals and special events further elevate the island's nightlife, creating unforgettable memories for those lucky enough to visit at the right time. Carnival, with its parades, costumes, and music-filled streets, is the most iconic celebration, but throughout the year, Martinique hosts music festivals, cultural gatherings, and dance nights that showcase both traditional and modern influences. During these times, the nightlife expands beyond bars and clubs, transforming the entire island into a stage where joy and rhythm are shared by everyone.

For those who prefer quieter evenings, Martinique also offers options for refined nights out. Elegant restaurants often feature live piano or acoustic music, providing a more intimate atmosphere for couples or travelers looking for relaxation. Jazz bars in particular are popular, where skilled musicians blend local traditions with international influences in a sophisticated yet approachable setting. These spaces reflect Martinique's ability to cater to a wide spectrum of tastes, from high-energy dance parties to gentle nights of music and conversation.

Nightlife in Martinique is not just about venues or genres; it is about the communal experience of coming together. Whether you are dancing to zouk in a crowded club, swaying to reggae by the beach, or sharing stories with locals over rum and laughter, the evenings invite you to be part of something larger. They allow travelers to see beyond the daylight beauty of the island and to experience the living culture that defines Martinique's heart.

Ultimately, exploring nightlife and live music in Martinique is as much a part of discovering the island as hiking its mountains or swimming in its turquoise waters. It is a celebration of heritage, creativity, and the joy of connection, offering moments that remain vivid long after the trip has ended. From vibrant clubs to relaxed beach gatherings, every night on the island carries its own rhythm, inviting you to step into Martinique's spirit and dance your way into its story.

Chapter 10

Culture, History & Heritage

Colonial Landmarks & Museums

Colonial landmarks and museums in Martinique offer an extraordinary window into the island's layered history, a history shaped by indigenous peoples, European colonization, the transatlantic slave trade, and the blending of cultures that continues to define Martinique today. For travelers seeking a deeper understanding of the island beyond its natural beauty, these cultural sites provide essential context. They reveal how Martinique became what it is today, not only through architecture and artifacts but also through the resilience and creativity of its people. Exploring them allows you to journey into Martinique's past while appreciating the richness of its heritage in the present.

The capital, Fort-de-France, is the island's cultural heart and home to some of its most striking colonial-era architecture. The Schoelcher Library stands as one of the most iconic landmarks, both for its beauty and its symbolic significance. Designed in Paris and shipped in pieces to Martinique in the late nineteenth century, the building honors Victor Schoelcher, the French abolitionist who played a central role in ending slavery in the French colonies. Its eclectic design, combining Byzantine, Art Nouveau, and Egyptian influences, immediately captures attention, while inside it houses an important collection of historical works, many donated by Schoelcher himself. For visitors, it is more than just a library, it is a monument to knowledge, freedom, and the enduring value of cultural preservation.

Another remarkable structure in Fort-de-France is St. Louis Cathedral, whose spire rises above the city. The cathedral has been rebuilt several times after earthquakes, fires, and hurricanes, with its current version dating to the late nineteenth century.

Built with iron framework by the same architect who worked on the Eiffel Tower's design, the cathedral is an architectural marvel. Its stained-glass windows, wooden details, and imposing presence are reminders of the colonial period's religious influence, while also showing how Martinique's faith traditions merged with African and Creole practices to form a unique cultural identity.

Museums across the island provide equally valuable insight into Martinique's history. The Musée de la Pagerie, located near Trois-Îlets, is the childhood home of Joséphine de Beauharnais, who later became Empress of France as the wife of Napoleon Bonaparte. The small museum offers a glimpse into her early life on the island, displaying personal items, documents, and relics that connect the Caribbean colony to European history. Visiting the Pagerie estate allows travelers to imagine life on a sugar plantation, while also prompting reflection on the human stories both privileged and enslaved that existed within these spaces.

For a more direct confrontation with the realities of colonialism and slavery, the Musée de la Mer et de l'Escalavage in Le Diamant is an essential stop. This museum focuses on the transatlantic slave trade and its impact on Martinique and the wider Caribbean. Through artifacts, documents, and multimedia exhibits, it traces the suffering, resistance, and ultimate contributions of enslaved Africans to the island's culture. It is a sobering but necessary visit, one that deepens understanding of Martinique's identity and honors the memory of those who endured unimaginable hardship.

Another moving site is Anse Cafard Slave Memorial, an open-air monument in Le Diamant overlooking the sea. The memorial consists of fifteen massive white stone statues, positioned in a triangular formation facing the water. It commemorates a tragic shipwreck in 1830, when a slave ship ran aground and hundreds of enslaved Africans lost their lives. The memorial is haunting in its silence, inviting reflection and remembrance, and for many visitors, it becomes one of the most powerful experiences of their time in Martinique.

The island also preserves its history through smaller museums that highlight specific aspects of heritage. The Musée de la Banane near Sainte-Marie explores the story of the banana, both as a key agricultural crop and as a symbol of Martinique's economy. The Musée du Rhum, meanwhile, combines history with one of the island's most iconic exports, rum, allowing visitors to learn about its production through the centuries. Each of these places emphasizes how agriculture, trade, and colonial policies shaped daily life and continue to influence Martinique's economy and culture.

Colonial forts also mark the island's landscape and narrate the struggles of empire. Fort Saint Louis in Fort-de-France, still an active military base, offers tours that reveal its strategic role in defending the island. With sweeping views over the bay, its ramparts and cannons evoke centuries of naval battles and colonial rivalries. Similarly, smaller fortifications around the coast remind visitors that Martinique's position in the Caribbean made it both a prize and a battleground for European powers.

What makes these landmarks and museums so compelling is not just their architectural beauty or collections but the stories they embody. Together, they chart the journey from colonization and slavery to abolition, from hardship to resilience, and from division to cultural synthesis. They also remind us that Martinique's identity is complex, blending African, European, and indigenous influences into something uniquely its own. For travelers, visiting these sites is a chance not only to learn but to engage meaningfully with the island's past and to see how that past continues to shape the present.

Exploring colonial landmarks and museums in Martinique ultimately adds layers of depth to any journey. They balance the island's beaches and mountains with a profound sense of place, showing that Martinique is not only a destination of natural wonders but also a land of memory, creativity, and survival. For anyone who wishes to go beyond surface impressions and truly know the island, these cultural sites are indispensable stops, each adding a piece to the larger mosaic of Martinique's heritage.

Afro-Caribbean Traditions

Afro-Caribbean traditions are at the very heart of Martinique's cultural identity, shaping not only the island's music, dance, and festivals but also its food, spirituality, language, and everyday way of life. While the island bears the imprint of French colonial rule and European influence, it is the deep and enduring heritage of Africa, carried across the Atlantic during the era of slavery, that gives Martinique its soul. These traditions have survived centuries of hardship, adapted to new circumstances, and blended with European and indigenous elements to create a vibrant Creole culture that continues to thrive today. For travelers seeking a deeper understanding of Martinique, immersing themselves in Afro-Caribbean traditions is one of the most rewarding ways to connect with the island's living heritage.

One of the most visible expressions of this heritage is music. Drumming, in particular, carries immense cultural weight in Martinique, not only as a form of entertainment but also as a connection to ancestral practices. The traditional bèlè drum, played while dancers perform barefoot on the earth, represents one of the island's oldest Afro-Caribbean art forms. Originating among enslaved Africans, the bèlè was once a form of resistance and community expression, performed secretly in rural gatherings and tied to agricultural rhythms and communal celebrations. Today, bèlè is both preserved and celebrated through festivals, performances, and dance classes, where locals and visitors can experience the hypnotic blend of call-and-response singing, rhythmic drumming, and expressive movement that define this tradition. It is often described as the heartbeat of Martinique, a cultural form that survived despite attempts to suppress it during colonial times.

Carnival in Martinique is another Afro-Caribbean tradition that showcases the creativity and resilience of the island's people. Rooted in European pre-Lenten celebrations but transformed through African influence, Carnival is an explosion of music, dance, and masquerade. Costumes often carry symbolic meanings, blending satire, resistance, and cultural pride. The characters of

Carnival such as the fearsome red devil figures or the elaborately dressed queens embody the fusion of African and Creole storytelling with festive spirit. The streets of Fort-de-France and smaller towns come alive with parades, steel drum bands, and dancing that continues late into the night. Beyond its joyful atmosphere, Carnival is also a statement of identity, where Afro-Caribbean traditions are proudly displayed as a defining part of Martinique's culture.

Spiritual practices in Martinique also bear the strong imprint of African heritage, particularly in the form of syncretic religions that blend Catholicism with African beliefs. While the island is predominantly Catholic, Afro-Caribbean traditions live on in folk practices, healing rituals, and ceremonies that preserve a connection to African cosmology. Herbal medicine, spiritual chants, and rituals for protection or good fortune are still practiced in rural areas, handed down through generations. This blending of faiths shows how African traditions adapted within the constraints of colonial society, creating a uniquely Creole spiritual landscape. For visitors, even if these practices are not always publicly visible, their influence can be sensed in festivals, ceremonies, and the everyday importance of community ties.

Language itself is another crucial element of Afro-Caribbean traditions in Martinique. While French is the official language, Martinican Creole is spoken widely across the island and carries the rhythms and vocabulary of African languages, combined with French, Carib, and other linguistic influences. Creole developed as a way for enslaved Africans from diverse regions to communicate with one another and with Europeans, and over time it became a cornerstone of cultural identity. Today, Creole is not only spoken but also celebrated in literature, poetry, theater, and music, serving as a vibrant expression of Afro-Caribbean heritage. For travelers, learning even a few phrases of Creole is a meaningful way to engage with local people and show appreciation for the island's cultural roots.

Dance in Martinique, much like music, is deeply tied to Afro-Caribbean traditions. Beyond the bèlè, other dance forms such as the mazurka and biguine reflect the blending of African rhythms with European structures. The biguine, in particular, became a symbol of Martinican identity in the nineteenth century, spreading even to Paris where it influenced broader musical trends. These dances are more than performances; they are acts of cultural continuity, expressing joy, resilience, and community spirit. Attending a local dance event or festival gives travelers the chance to see how these traditions continue to evolve while staying grounded in their African origins.

Food also reflects Afro-Caribbean heritage, with ingredients and cooking methods that trace back to Africa. Dishes like accras (salt cod fritters), callaloo soup, and richly spiced stews highlight the African contribution to Martinique's culinary traditions. Cassava, yams, okra, and plantains, all staples of African diets, remain central in Martinican kitchens. Meals are often communal, echoing the African tradition of food as a binding force within families and communities. Combined with influences from indigenous peoples and French cuisine, the Afro-Caribbean foundation of Martinique's food culture is unmistakable, making every dish part of the island's living history.

Festivals and cultural events often serve as the most accessible way for visitors to experience Afro-Caribbean traditions firsthand. In addition to Carnival, the annual Festival Bèlè brings together musicians, dancers, and scholars to celebrate the bèlè tradition, while events highlighting Creole language, storytelling, and cuisine emphasize the enduring vitality of Afro-Caribbean culture. These gatherings are not staged performances for tourists but rather authentic expressions of identity, often drawing large local crowds who come together to honor their heritage.

What makes Afro-Caribbean traditions in Martinique particularly powerful is the way they embody survival and adaptation. Born out of the brutal history of slavery and colonization, these traditions were acts of resilience for enslaved Africans to preserve their humanity, share their stories, and build community. Over centuries, they became the foundation of a Creole identity that embraces diversity and celebrates creativity. For visitors, engaging with these traditions is not only about appreciating vibrant music or delicious food; it is about recognizing the depth of history and the strength of a culture that refused to be erased.

In experiencing Afro-Caribbean traditions, travelers gain a richer, more meaningful connection to Martinique. They discover that the island's beauty lies not only in its beaches and mountains but also in the rhythms of its drums, the flavor of its food, the energy of its dances, and the pride of its people in their heritage. By seeking out these traditions whether at a village festival, a dance performance, or through everyday encounters with local people visitors step into the living story of Martinique, a story shaped by Africa, adapted in the Caribbean, and celebrated with joy and resilience.

Arts, Crafts & Local Markets

Arts, crafts, and local markets in Martinique are more than just points of interest for visitors; they are living expressions of the island's culture, history, and heritage. Every handmade object, every stall filled with bright textiles or hand-carved wooden figures, and every jar of local spices sold in the market reflects centuries of creativity, resilience, and adaptation. To explore Martinique's arts and markets is to gain a deeper understanding of its Creole identity, shaped by African, European, and indigenous influences, yet distinctly Caribbean in style and spirit. For travelers who want to experience the island beyond its natural beauty, immersing themselves in its artisanal traditions and vibrant marketplaces is a direct connection to the daily life and cultural heartbeat of Martinique.

The roots of Martinique's artistic traditions can be traced back to the fusion of cultures that define the island. African heritage introduced techniques in weaving, carving, and pottery, while French colonial presence brought European styles, and indigenous Arawak and Carib peoples contributed knowledge of local materials and decorative patterns. Over time, these elements merged into a distinctive Creole style that is visible in the arts and crafts of today. From colorful madras fabric to handwoven baskets and pottery that blends functional utility with artistic expression, these creations embody the layered history of the island.

One of the most iconic elements of Martinican culture is the use of madras fabric, a brightly colored, plaid cotton material that has come to symbolize Creole identity. Originally imported from India by way of European trade, madras became a staple in Caribbean dress and was adapted by local communities to create vibrant clothing, headscarves, and decorative items. In Martinique, madras is often seen in traditional costumes, particularly during festivals, weddings, and cultural celebrations. Women wear it as head wraps, often tied in elaborate styles that once carried symbolic messages about their marital status. Today, artisans continue to produce and sell madras textiles in markets, and visitors can purchase not only clothing but also accessories, table linens, and decorative items made from this cultural fabric.

Basket weaving is another deeply rooted craft that has survived and thrived in Martinique. Using local materials such as larouma reeds or bamboo, artisans create baskets, mats, hats, and household objects that are both practical and beautiful. Basket weaving was once an essential skill for daily life on the island, providing storage for food, tools, and personal items. Though modern alternatives exist, the craft continues as a proud tradition, with artisans often demonstrating their techniques at markets and cultural events. For visitors, purchasing a handwoven basket is not just acquiring a souvenir but taking home a piece of living heritage that connects to the resourcefulness and artistry of past generations.

Wood carving also occupies a special place in Martinique's artisanal culture. Skilled craftsmen carve intricate figures, masks, utensils, and decorative objects from local woods, often incorporating motifs that reflect African and Creole traditions. Some carvings depict human figures or spiritual symbols, linking back to ancestral practices and cultural storytelling. Others are purely decorative, showcasing the natural beauty of Caribbean woods and the artisan's craftsmanship. In markets and artisan workshops, travelers can witness the creativity and dedication that goes into these works, each piece carrying with it the cultural memory of the island.

Pottery and ceramics are equally important in Martinique's craft traditions. Clay from the island is shaped into both functional household items and decorative art pieces. Historically, pottery was vital for cooking and storage, but it also provided a creative outlet for artisans who decorated their work with unique patterns and designs. Today, Martinican pottery often blends traditional techniques with contemporary aesthetics, making it popular among collectors and visitors alike. Many workshops welcome guests, allowing them to watch artisans at work or purchase one-of-a-kind pieces directly from the makers.

Local markets serve as the primary stage where these arts and crafts come together, alongside the vibrant exchange of food, spices, and daily goods. The Grand Marché in Fort-de-France is perhaps the most famous, offering a sensory feast of colors, sounds, and aromas. Visitors strolling through the market will find stalls overflowing with tropical fruits, handmade crafts, medicinal herbs, bottles of spiced rum, and colorful textiles. Artisans sell their creations directly, giving travelers the chance to speak with them, learn about their techniques, and understand the cultural significance of their work. Smaller markets in towns and villages across the island also provide more intimate settings, where the rhythm of daily life is more apparent and the relationship between producers and community is tangible.

Markets are also places of cultural exchange, where oral traditions, recipes, and knowledge are passed down. Vendors often tell stories of how a craft was taught to them by parents or grandparents, highlighting the role of markets as spaces where heritage is actively transmitted from one generation to the next. Beyond commerce, markets function as social hubs, where music may play in the background, people gather to chat, and traditions are kept alive through the simple act of meeting and sharing.

For travelers, engaging with arts, crafts, and markets in Martinique provides an authentic way to support local communities. Buying directly from artisans ensures that traditional skills remain viable and that cultural heritage continues to be valued. Many artisans take pride not only in selling their creations but also in sharing the history behind them, whether it is the story of madras fabric, the meaning of a carved figure, or the techniques of weaving baskets from reeds. This exchange creates connections between visitors and locals that go beyond transactions, enriching the travel experience with cultural depth.

The influence of Afro-Caribbean heritage is visible in nearly all forms of Martinique's artistic expression, from the motifs in paintings and carvings to the colors of fabrics and market displays. Modern artists on the island often draw inspiration from these traditions, blending them with contemporary techniques to create works that speak both to the past and to the present. Galleries in Fort-de-France and cultural centers around the island showcase this evolution, demonstrating how Martinique's heritage continues to inspire creativity in new forms.

In exploring arts, crafts, and local markets, visitors not only encounter the tangible beauty of handmade objects but also step into the intangible world of heritage, where stories, skills, and cultural pride are preserved. Each object carries with it the imprint of history, each market stall embodies community life, and each purchase supports the continuation of traditions that might otherwise be lost in a rapidly changing world.

Chapter 11

Build Your Perfect Itinerary

A 3-Day Quick Escape

A three-day quick escape to Martinique is a wonderful way to sample the island's diverse offerings, blending cultural discovery, natural beauty, and culinary indulgence into a short yet memorable journey. While three days cannot possibly capture all that Martinique has to offer, it allows visitors to experience a thoughtful balance of city life, coastal relaxation, and lush interior landscapes. By structuring each day around different aspects of the island its history, its beaches, and its natural adventures travelers can enjoy an itinerary that feels both complete and inspiring, leaving them with the desire to return for a longer stay in the future.

The first day of this short escape should focus on Fort-de-France, the bustling capital city and the heart of Martinique's cultural and historical life. Begin with a visit to the Schoelcher Library, an architectural jewel designed by Henri Picq and shipped piece by piece from Paris in the nineteenth century. Its ornate ironwork and vibrant glass windows immediately reveal the blend of European elegance and Caribbean vitality that defines so much of Martinique. From there, stroll toward Saint-Louis Cathedral, whose striking Gothic-inspired architecture has stood the test of hurricanes and earthquakes, embodying resilience and faith. Just beyond, the city's markets beckon with a feast of colors and aromas. The Grand Marché is an essential stop, where vendors sell local spices like cinnamon, nutmeg, and cloves, as well as jars of spicy Creole sauces, bottles of rhum agricole, and baskets of fresh tropical fruits. This is not only a place to shop but also an opportunity to converse with locals and feel the pulse of daily life.

Lunch in Fort-de-France can introduce visitors to Martinican cuisine at its finest. Local restaurants serve traditional dishes such as accras de morue, which are crisp salt cod fritters, or a plate of colombo, a spiced curry-like stew of meat and vegetables that reflects the island's Indian influences. After lunch, head to the Jardin de Balata, located just a short drive outside the city. This botanical garden offers a serene introduction to Martinique's flora, with lush tropical plants, orchids, and tree-fern groves lining winding paths. Suspension bridges high in the canopy provide panoramic views of the surrounding mountains and forest, making it an unforgettable highlight of the first day. As the evening approaches, return to Fort-de-France for a sunset stroll along La Savane, the central park by the waterfront. Dotted with statues and overlooked by palm trees, it is a fitting place to reflect on the blend of history and modernity encountered on the first day. Dinner can be enjoyed at a waterfront restaurant, accompanied by a taste of local rum or ti' punch, Martinique's traditional cocktail.

The second day shifts focus to the beaches and coastal charm of the southern part of the island. Set out early toward Les Trois-Îlets, a resort area offering calm waters, golden sands, and a more relaxed pace. Begin with a visit to the Maison de la Canne, a museum housed in a former sugar factory that traces the history of sugarcane on the island, from its colonial plantation days to its role in modern rum production. The exhibits shed light on both the economic development of Martinique and the harsh realities of slavery and labor that built its wealth. From there, continue to Pointe du Bout, a lively area with boutiques, cafes, and a marina. This is an excellent spot to board a catamaran or boat excursion, many of which offer half-day sails along the coast, complete with snorkeling stops in crystal-clear waters teeming with tropical fish.

Lunch on the second day can be enjoyed seaside, with restaurants serving freshly caught fish, grilled lobster, and Creole sides such as fried plantains or breadfruit gratin. The afternoon can be devoted to pure relaxation at Anse Mitan or Anse à l'Ane, two popular beaches near Trois-Îlets. The calm waters are perfect for swimming, and the views across the bay toward Fort-de-France are stunning, especially in the late afternoon light. For those interested in art and history, La Pagerie, the childhood home of Empress Joséphine (Napoleon Bonaparte's first wife), offers a glimpse into Martinique's colonial past. The estate is now a museum with personal artifacts, period furniture, and exhibits that spark reflection on how one small Caribbean island shaped European history. As evening falls, dine at one of the beachside restaurants where the sound of waves accompanies the flavors of a Creole feast, making the second day both relaxing and enriching.

The third day is dedicated to Martinique's rugged natural beauty, offering adventure and scenery that contrasts with the island's urban and coastal sides. An early start is recommended for a drive north toward Mont Pelée, the towering volcano that dominates the northern landscape. This volcano famously erupted in 1902, destroying the town of Saint-Pierre and shaping the island's history forever. Today, Mont Pelée offers a variety of hiking trails ranging from moderate walks to challenging climbs, depending on fitness and interest. Even a shorter hike provides breathtaking views of the coastline, lush valleys, and the cloud-shrouded summit. For those not inclined to hike, the surrounding countryside itself is worth exploring, with its rolling hills, banana plantations, and small villages.

After a morning of exploration, descend toward Saint-Pierre, the town once known as the "Paris of the Caribbean." Though much of it was destroyed in the eruption, ruins such as the theater and the old prison remain as evocative reminders of the disaster. The Musée Volcanologique provides detailed exhibits about the eruption and its aftermath, offering context to the haunting ruins scattered throughout the town. Lunch in Saint-Pierre can be taken at a small local restaurant serving fresh seafood dishes, often accompanied by local vegetables like dasheen or cassava. The afternoon can continue with a visit to a rum distillery in the north, such as Depaz or Neisson, both of which offer tours that walk visitors through the process of making Martinique's famed rhum agricole. Tastings are usually included, allowing guests to appreciate the unique flavors derived from fresh sugarcane juice rather than molasses.

As the final evening approaches, travelers can return southward for a farewell dinner, perhaps choosing a spot with live music or traditional dance performances. The rhythms of zouk or biguine provide a lively and fitting end to the journey, reminding visitors that Martinique's culture is as vibrant and dynamic as its landscapes.

Though three days is a short window of time, this itinerary allows travelers to encounter the richness of Martinique from multiple perspectives: the history and culture of Fort-de-France, the beauty and leisure of the southern beaches, and the dramatic natural wonders of the north. It balances exploration with relaxation, creating a rhythm that feels immersive without being overwhelming. For many, such a quick escape becomes a first taste of

Martinique, sparking curiosity and a longing to return for a longer, deeper exploration.

A 7-Day Balanced Adventure

A seven-day adventure in Martinique allows travelers to experience the island's natural beauty, cultural richness, and relaxed Caribbean lifestyle without having to rush. It offers a balance between active exploration and peaceful downtime, creating space for adventure in the rainforest, immersion in Creole culture, and moments of relaxation on golden beaches. With a week at your disposal, you can cover both the north and south of the island, sampling mountain trails, volcanic scenery, fishing villages, and vibrant urban life while still leaving time to unwind. This kind of itinerary is ideal for those who want a comprehensive yet enjoyable introduction to Martinique.

Begin your week in Fort-de-France, the capital and cultural heart of the island. Spend your first day exploring its landmarks such as the Schoelcher Library, the lively markets filled with spices and tropical fruit, and the historic Fort Saint-Louis. This will give you an immediate sense of Martinique's French-Caribbean blend, from colonial architecture to bustling Creole street life. Enjoy a leisurely evening at one of the city's waterfront restaurants, where you can savor local seafood while watching the sunset over the bay. Starting here helps ground you in the island's heritage before venturing further afield.

On the second day, head north to experience Mount Pelée, Martinique's famous volcano. You don't need to attempt the summit unless you're a seasoned hiker, but even moderate trails offer sweeping views of lush valleys and coastal panoramas. Afterward, visit the town of Saint-Pierre, once the "Paris of the Caribbean," destroyed in the 1902 eruption. Its ruins, along with the Volcanological Museum, create a powerful connection to the island's history. In the afternoon, enjoy a relaxing drive through banana plantations and rainforests, stopping at scenic viewpoints or small villages that reveal Martinique's slower pace of life.

Day three can be devoted to the island's waterfalls and rainforest trails. The north is especially rich in natural wonders such as Cascade Didier or Saut du Gendarme, where the cool water is a reward after a shaded hike. Alternatively, explore the Balata Botanical Garden, where suspended bridges offer panoramic views of the rainforest canopy. This day is about immersing yourself in the lush, untamed side of Martinique, balancing the cultural depth of Fort-de-France with raw natural beauty.

With half of your week still ahead, turn toward the southern coast for a change of scenery. Day four is perfect for visiting Les Trois-Îlets, a resort town with strong cultural ties to the island's past. You can tour La Savane des Esclaves, an open-air museum dedicated to Creole history, then relax on nearby beaches such as Anse Mitan or Pointe du Bout. This is also an excellent base for a sunset boat excursion or a casual evening enjoying local nightlife, where rum cocktails and live zouk music create an unforgettable Caribbean atmosphere.

Day five invites exploration of Martinique's rum heritage. Spend time touring a plantation or distillery, such as Habitation Clément or Rhum J.M., where you'll learn how sugarcane transforms into the island's world-famous agricole rum. Tastings are often paired with stories about family traditions and Creole craftsmanship, making it more than just a drink but an immersion into heritage. In the afternoon, unwind at one of the south's quieter beaches like Grande Anse d'Arlet, a charming fishing village where colorful houses frame a tranquil bay perfect for snorkeling.

On day six, dedicate time to adventure on the water. Options include kayaking through mangroves, sailing along the coast, or taking a ferry to one of the smaller islets offshore. Snorkelers and divers will find coral reefs teeming with marine life, while those who prefer a more relaxed outing might enjoy a glass-bottom boat tour. This day emphasizes Martinique's identity as an island where land and sea offer equally enriching opportunities.

For your final day, allow yourself to slow down and savor Martinique's gentle rhythm. Spend the morning at a market, picking up spices, handmade crafts, or rum to bring home as souvenirs. Then retreat to a quiet beach or café where you can reflect on the experiences of the week. Whether you choose the lively Grande Anse du Diamant or a more secluded cove, this last day should be about soaking in the essence of the island, its warmth, colors, and spirit.

A seven-day balanced itinerary ensures that visitors see Martinique in its full dimension: a land of volcanic peaks and golden sands, of French refinement and Afro-Caribbean rhythms, of lively markets and serene villages. By weaving together culture, history, nature, and relaxation, it becomes more than a holiday; it transforms into a journey of discovery, with memories that linger long after departure. This rhythm of adventure and rest is what makes a week in Martinique truly fulfilling.

A 10-Day In-Depth Exploration

A ten-day journey through Martinique gives travelers the luxury of time, allowing for a truly in-depth exploration of the island's many layers. While shorter visits capture snapshots of Martinique, a longer stay opens the door to lingering in small fishing villages, taking unhurried hikes through the rainforest, diving deeper into Creole culture, and enjoying leisurely afternoons where the island's easy rhythm takes hold. With ten days, you can strike a harmonious balance between the island's north and south, its cultural richness and natural treasures, its bustling urban life and its quiet rural corners. This itinerary is designed for those who want to experience Martinique as more than just a beach getaway, creating a well-rounded adventure that touches every dimension of the island.

Begin your exploration in Fort-de-France, where days one and two provide the perfect foundation. Spend your first day wandering through the Schoelcher Library, the St. Louis Cathedral, and the bustling covered market that brims with spices, fresh produce, and souvenirs that reflect everyday Martinican life. An afternoon stroll along waterfront or a relaxed dinner by the bay offers an introduction to the island's flavors and atmosphere. On the second day, explore the Balata Botanical

Garden, a lush sanctuary that showcases the island's flora, with canopy walkways and sweeping views over the hills. Pair this with a visit to Sacré-Cœur de Balata, a church inspired by Montmartre in Paris, standing like a sentinel above the rainforest. These first days set the cultural and natural stage for what lies ahead.

Day three brings you into the northern reaches, where Mount Pelée dominates the landscape. Whether you hike part of its slopes or simply explore the surrounding villages, this day is about encountering the untamed wilderness of Martinique. The town of Saint-Pierre, once a thriving cultural capital, lies at the base of the volcano, and its ruins serve as a haunting reminder of the 1902 eruption. A visit to the Volcanological Museum deepens the sense of history, while the charm of local cafés allows for reflection on how life has been rebuilt.

On day four, dedicate yourself to waterfalls and rainforest trails. Saut du Gendarme or Cascade Didier are excellent options for a refreshing hike followed by a swim in clear pools. These experiences immerse travelers in the sensory richness of the island: the scent of damp earth, the chorus of tropical birds, and the cool rush of mountain streams. If time permits, a drive along the northern Atlantic coast offers dramatic views of cliffs and black-sand beaches, giving the sense of being at the edge of the wild Caribbean.

The fifth day transitions you toward culture and history, making Les Trois-Îlets an ideal base. Here, you can spend the morning exploring La Savane des Esclaves, an open-air museum that recounts Martinique's past with poignant exhibits on slavery, Creole traditions, and everyday rural life. The afternoon can be devoted to relaxation on the beaches of Anse Mitan or Pointe du Bout, both of which combine natural beauty with lively waterfront cafés. Evenings in this area often include live music, offering a chance to experience zouk rhythms and Creole hospitality firsthand.

Day six is devoted to Martinique's rum heritage, an essential part of the island's cultural identity. Habitation Clément and Rhum J.M. are just two of the distilleries where you can learn about agricole rum production and taste its unique character. These visits often include tours of the plantations, elegant estates, and historic cellars, making it a cultural as well as culinary experience. Pair this with a leisurely lunch featuring Creole classics such as accras or colombo, and you have a day that unites history, craftsmanship, and flavor.

Day seven offers the opportunity for outdoor adventure at sea. Options include sailing excursions that reveal hidden coves and offshore islets, kayaking through mangroves that shelter exotic birds, or snorkeling in the calm waters near Anse Dufour, where sea turtles are often spotted. This day emphasizes the island's relationship with the sea, reminding travelers that Martinique is not only a place of mountains and forests but also an aquatic paradise.

With three more days at your disposal, you can go even deeper into the southern half of the island. Day eight might take you to Le Diamant, where the Diamond Rock juts dramatically out of the sea. The town itself offers cultural history tied to battles between French and British forces, while nearby Grande Anse du Diamant provides a sweeping beach perfect for a long walk or an afternoon of sun. Combine this with a visit to Cap 110, a moving memorial dedicated to the memory of enslaved Africans, which anchors the day in reflection as well as relaxation.

On day nine, explore the wilder Atlantic side of the island, where wind and waves shape the coastline. The Presqu'île de la Caravelle is a nature reserve with trails that wind through mangroves, savannas, and dramatic coastal cliffs. The hike here is both invigorating and scenic, with the ruins of Château Dubuc offering a glimpse into the island's colonial past. This is one of Martinique's best places to experience both biodiversity and history in a single outing, rewarding those who venture away from the well-trodden south coast.

Finally, day ten should be unhurried, devoted to savoring the island before departure. Begin with a market visit, perhaps in Fort-de-France or a smaller town, to pick up spices, rum, or handcrafted souvenirs. Spend your afternoon on a favorite beach—whether the bustling sands of Les Anses-d'Arlet or a quieter cove discovered earlier in your journey. The evening can be reserved for one last Creole feast, where music and conversation flow as easily as the island's warm hospitality. This final day is less about doing than about being, letting the spirit of Martinique linger as you prepare to leave.

A ten-day itinerary in Martinique allows for the fullest expression of the island's character. It gives time for exploration of its northern mountains and southern beaches, for immersion in Afro-Caribbean traditions and French-inspired refinement, for tasting rum at its source and savoring Creole meals prepared with love. With each day flowing into the next, the island becomes more than a destination; it becomes a lived experience, one where adventure, history, and leisure blend seamlessly into a journey that feels both expansive and intimate. Those who allow themselves ten days will leave not only with photographs and souvenirs but with a deeper connection to Martinique's soul.

Conclusion

Final Travel Tips

As your journey through Martinique comes to a close, it is helpful to carry with you a collection of final travel tips that will not only ease your visit but also enrich it. A place as layered and multifaceted as Martinique reveals itself most beautifully when travelers arrive prepared yet open-minded, ready to embrace both the expected and the unexpected. These final notes serve as a guide to help you navigate the island with confidence, sensitivity, and joy, ensuring that every moment is as fulfilling as possible.

One of the first things to remember when visiting Martinique is that it is a blend of French and Caribbean influences. This duality shapes everything from the language to the cuisine, from infrastructure to cultural rhythms. French is the official language, and while many people in tourism speak some English, learning a few simple French phrases such as greetings, polite expressions, and basic questions can go a long way in creating warmth during interactions. Beyond French, Martinicans also speak Creole, which is part of their identity and heritage, so showing curiosity and respect for this language demonstrates cultural sensitivity. Even if you only master a few words, your effort will be appreciated.

Practical considerations such as money, transportation, and timing also deserve attention. The currency is the euro, and while credit cards are widely accepted, it is always useful to carry some cash for smaller purchases, local markets, or rural areas. ATMs are available across the island, but in less populated regions, they may not be as frequent, so withdrawing ahead of time is wise. Driving is the best way to explore Martinique's diverse landscapes, from volcanic mountains to secluded beaches. Roads are generally well maintained, but they can be winding and narrow, especially in the northern part of the island, so patience and caution are recommended. Renting a car also gives the freedom to discover less accessible places, such as hidden coves or hilltop villages, at your own pace.

Packing for Martinique should balance practicality with comfort. Lightweight clothing suitable for the tropical climate is essential, along with swimwear, sandals, and breathable fabrics. However, you will also want to bring sturdy shoes for hiking, as the island's trails lead through rainforests, over volcanic terrain, and along coastal paths. A light jacket or sweater may be useful in the evenings or when exploring higher altitudes around Mount Pelée. Sun protection is vital: sunscreen, a wide-brimmed hat, and sunglasses will help guard against the strong Caribbean sun, while insect repellent is recommended for forested areas or evenings outdoors.

When it comes to food and drink, Martinique offers experiences that are as much a part of your journey as the landscapes. From Creole street snacks such as accras (fried cod fritters) to refined French-Caribbean fusion dishes in restaurants, tasting your way through the island is an adventure in itself. Fresh fruit, tropical juices, and locally caught seafood are staples of daily life. Rum, especially agricole rum distilled from fresh sugarcane juice, is not only a drink but also a cultural expression of the island. Exploring distilleries gives insight into its production and history, and tastings reveal its complexity. A tip to keep in mind is that meals in Martinique often follow French dining rhythms, with a slower pace and multiple courses, so allow yourself to enjoy the ritual rather than rushing through.

Respect for the local culture and environment is another important element of travel here. Martinique is a place of proud heritage, where traditions, music, and daily life reflect centuries of resilience and creativity. Attending a festival, watching a dance performance, or simply striking up a conversation with locals are ways to connect meaningfully. At the same time, be mindful of environmental responsibility. The island's natural beauty is one of its greatest treasures, so taking care to avoid littering, respecting hiking trails, and using reef-safe sunscreen to protect marine life are simple yet powerful ways to contribute to its preservation.

Timing your trip well can also enhance the experience. High season runs from December to April, when the weather is warm and dry, making it ideal for outdoor activities. This period coincides with Carnival, one of Martinique's most vibrant cultural events, which is worth experiencing if your schedule allows. The summer and early autumn months tend to be hotter and more humid, with a higher chance of rain or storms, but they also offer fewer crowds and a more tranquil atmosphere. Each season brings its own character, so consider what balance of activity, relaxation, and cultural events fits your preferences.

Finally, one of the most rewarding tips is to allow yourself the flexibility to slow down. While it is tempting to plan every day full of sights and activities, Martinique reveals its heart when you take the time to linger whether sitting in a café in Fort-de-France, watching the fishermen return with their catch, or strolling along the shoreline as the sun sets. These unplanned moments often become the most treasured memories. The island is not just a destination of sights but a place of atmosphere, where rhythms of the sea, music, and community create a living tapestry.

In conclusion, traveling through Martinique is both an exploration and a dialogue between past and present, between nature and culture, between visitor and local. By arriving prepared with practical knowledge, showing respect for traditions, savoring its culinary delights, and taking time to appreciate its natural wonders, you give yourself the chance to experience the island in a way that is both meaningful and unforgettable. These final travel tips are not simply about convenience; they are about approaching Martinique with openness, curiosity, and care, ensuring that your journey leaves you enriched while leaving the island just as beautiful for those who follow.

Why Martinique Stays With You

As you prepare to leave Martinique, you may find that the island lingers with you in ways that are difficult to fully put into words. This is not simply a destination where you take photographs, check off sights, and move on; it is a place that imprints itself on your senses, your spirit, and your memory. The true magic of Martinique is that it does not fade when the plane takes off or when you step back into your daily life. Instead, its rhythms, flavors, and colors remain with you, woven into your personal story of travel.

The first element that stays with you is the natural beauty of Martinique. From the moment you set eyes on the emerald peaks of Mount Pelée, the lush forests of the north, or the golden sands of Les Salines, you are immersed in an environment that feels alive and ever-changing. The island's landscapes are not just backdrops but experiences in themselves. The sound of waves rolling onto quiet beaches, the rush of waterfalls hidden in the jungle, and the sight of fishing boats bobbing on turquoise waters all find their way into your memory. Long after leaving, you will recall the salty breeze on your skin, the scent of blooming tropical flowers, and the sight of sunsets melting into the Caribbean horizon. Nature here has a way of reminding you how small you are within something vast, and that awareness is both grounding and unforgettable.

Equally powerful are the cultural encounters you experience. Martinique is a place where history, heritage, and creativity shape daily life. The Afro-Caribbean traditions, the rhythms of zouk and bèlè, the energy of Carnival, and the pride in Creole identity all leave an impression that goes far beyond the surface. You may not remember every detail of a festival or every word spoken in French or Creole, but you will remember the feeling of inclusion, of being welcomed into something larger than yourself. This sense of cultural depth rooted in resilience and joy creates an emotional connection that many visitors carry with them long after their journey.

Food and drink also leave a lasting mark. Tasting Martinique is like discovering a new language for the senses. You will recall the spice of Creole stews, the crunch of fresh accras, the sweetness of tropical fruit, and the depth of rum aged under the Caribbean sun. Meals are not just nourishment here; they are experiences, celebrations of life and identity. Even back home, a sip of rum or the aroma of grilled fish might instantly bring you back to a small seaside restaurant where laughter, music, and ocean breezes made the moment feel timeless.

Perhaps one of the strongest reasons Martinique stays with you is the warmth of its people. There is a generosity and pride that shines through in daily interactions, whether you are buying fruit from a market vendor, asking directions from a passerby, or talking with locals at a beachside café. These moments of connection, even brief ones, have a way of leaving their mark. Martinique is not just a place of landscapes and traditions but a community of people whose energy is inseparable from the identity of the island.

There is also something to be said for the island's contrasts and balance. Martinique carries both French refinement and Caribbean soul, modern conveniences and ancient traditions, bustling towns and tranquil hideaways. It invites you to explore and to relax, to seek adventure and to sit still. This harmony of opposites is rare, and it makes Martinique not just a holiday but a meditation on the beauty of diversity and coexistence. The island teaches you that life can be both vibrant and peaceful, both rooted and ever-evolving.

Finally, what lingers most is the way Martinique changes you as a traveler. When you have hiked through volcanic trails, wandered colorful markets, danced to island rhythms, and tasted the richness of Creole cuisine, you are not quite the same person as when you arrived. The island opens your eyes to the power of cultural fusion, the resilience of people shaped by history, and the simple joys of life lived close to the sea. It reminds you that travel is not only about discovery but also about transformation.

In the end, Martinique stays with you because it touches every part of the traveler's experience body, mind, and soul. It is the color of the waters, the pulse of the music, the taste of the food, the embrace of the culture, and the welcome of the people. Long after your visit, you may find yourself daydreaming of its beaches, replaying its songs in your mind, or yearning for the rhythm of its days. This is the gift of Martinique: it does not let you leave untouched. It stays with you quietly, like a gentle rhythm in the background of your life, calling you to return whenever you are ready to once again lose yourself in its beauty and rediscover its spirit.

Inspiration for Your Next Journey

Every great journey leaves a mark on the traveler, and Martinique is no exception. This island, with its lush green mountains, sun-drenched beaches, and soulful culture, is the kind of place that sparks not only memories but also a desire for more. As your time in Martinique comes to a close, you may feel a mixture of contentment and yearning, the joy of having experienced something remarkable, and the pull of knowing that the world still holds so many places, stories, and moments waiting for you to discover. The inspiration you carry from Martinique is not confined to this island; it is a reminder of the boundless opportunities that travel offers.

One of the most powerful ways Martinique inspires your next journey is by showing you the richness that comes from cultural fusion. Here, you experienced a blending of French sophistication with Afro-Caribbean traditions, a combination that creates something unique and vibrant. This lesson can inspire you to seek out other destinations where cultures meet and evolve together, where history has shaped traditions into something original, and where diversity itself becomes a form of beauty. Perhaps it will draw you toward other Caribbean islands with their own personalities, or maybe to distant places where cultures mix in surprising ways. The awareness that identity is not fixed but ever-changing may spark curiosity for future travels.

Martinique also reminds you of the importance of slowing down and living fully in the moment. Whether you were savoring a long meal by the sea, strolling through a market alive with colors and scents, or standing on a quiet beach at sunset, the island taught you that travel is not about rushing from one landmark to the next. It is about immersing yourself, taking in the details, and allowing your senses to be filled. This mindset can inspire your next journeys, encouraging you to seek places where you can experience not just the sights but the rhythms of daily life. You may find yourself longing for destinations where hospitality is heartfelt, meals are long, and life is celebrated not in grand gestures but in simple joys.

Nature in Martinique also leaves you with a thirst for further adventure. The volcanic peaks, coral reefs, mangrove swamps, and waterfalls remind you of how vast and varied the natural world is. They awaken a sense of wonder that calls you to explore new landscapes whether hiking through rainforests in another part of the world, snorkeling in new waters rich with marine life, or standing on mountain ridges with views that stretch into infinity. Martinique proves that nature is never something you simply pass by; it is something you enter into, something that changes you when you give yourself to it fully. That awareness can shape your future travels, guiding you to places where landscapes inspire the same awe and respect.

The island's art of celebration can also be carried forward as inspiration. In Martinique, music and dance flow through daily life, festivals bring people together in vibrant joy, and traditions are shared with pride. Experiencing these moments reminds you that travel is not only about seeing but also about feeling. It may inspire you to seek out destinations where local festivals pulse with energy, where music is a living expression of culture, and where communities open their arms to visitors as participants, not just observers. Carrying that spirit with you, you may find that your future journeys are not just about sights but about shared experiences that stay alive in your heart.

The flavors of Martinique also awaken a curiosity that can shape your future travel plans. The spice of Creole cuisine, the freshness of tropical fruits, the richness of local rums all remind you that food is one of the most profound ways to connect with a culture. This might inspire you to choose future destinations with culinary traditions that surprise and delight you, whether through street food, family recipes, or celebrated restaurants. The act of sitting down at a table in a new place becomes not just about eating, but about tasting history, geography, and identity all at once.

And finally, Martinique inspires by reminding you of the human connections at the heart of travel. The warmth of its people, the conversations shared even in fragments of French or Creole, and the kindness extended in small but meaningful ways highlight the fact that travel is ultimately about relationships. This awareness might lead you to seek out destinations where people, not monuments, become the highlight of your journey. It may remind you to remain open, curious, and humble wherever you go, ready to learn not only from the land but from those who live upon it.

As you look ahead, the inspiration of Martinique becomes a compass. It reminds you that your journeys should seek balance between discovery and rest, between adventure and reflection, between nature and culture. It teaches you to value authenticity, to linger in places long enough to truly feel them, and to travel not as an observer but as a participant in the world's endless stories.

Your next journey could take you anywhere: to another Caribbean island alive with music and color, to the historic cities of Europe, to the deserts and mountains of faraway continents. Wherever you go, the lessons and memories of Martinique will guide you. They will encourage you to listen more deeply, taste more boldly, move more slowly, and embrace more fully.

The island is a reminder that travel is not only about seeing new places but about becoming new yourself. Martinique stays with you, not to keep you tied to its shores, but to inspire you to keep moving forward, always seeking, always open, and always ready for the next adventure. With Martinique in your heart, every future journey becomes not just a trip, but a continuation of the story you began here: one of connection, discovery, and the endless beauty of the world.

Printed in Dunstable, United Kingdom